# STRIPS 'n Curves

## A New Spin on Strip Piecing

# LOUISA L. SMITH

C&T PUBLISHING

Copyright © 2001 Louisa L. Smith
Development Editor: Cyndy Lyle Rymer
Technical Editor: Karyn Hoyt
Copy Editor: Carol Barrett
Cover Design & Production: Kristen Yenche
Design Director/Book Designer: Kristen Yenche
Production Coordination: Diane Pedersen
Production Assistant: Stephanie Muir
Graphic Illustrations: Richard Sheppard
Cover Image: *Cycloid II*, 45$^1$/$_2$" x 37",
Louisa L. Smith, 1995. Photo by John Gasior
All photography by John Gasior unless otherwise noted.

Attention Teachers:
C&T Publishing, Inc. encourages you to use this
book as a text for teaching. Contact us at 800-
284-1114 or www.ctpub.com for more information
about the C&T Teachers Program.

Library of Congress Cataloging-in-Publication Data
Smith, Louisa L.

   Strips 'n curves : a new spin on strip piecing / Louisa
L. Smith.

      p. cm.
ISBN 1-57120-168-8

   1. Quilting--Patterns. 2. Strip quilting--Patterns. I. Title.

   TT835 .S564 2001

   746.46'041--dc21

                              2001002036

Published by C&T Publishing, Inc.
P.O. Box 1456
Lafayette, California 94549
Printed in China
10  9  8  7  6  5  4  3  2

## ACKNOWLEDGMENTS

I extend my sincere thanks to all my friends and students whose enthusiasm and hard work have helped and guided me through this process. A special thanks to my editors, Cyndy Rymer, Peggy Kass, and Karyn Hoyt, for their knowledge and guidance. My profound appreciation and thanks go to my husband Fred, my mom, my children Lisa and Michael, and my dear friend Anna, for their continued support. Without them this book would not now be in the hands of many eager quilters.

A special thanks to Viking Sewing Machines for giving me the opportunity to discover the incredible world of the Designer I; I honestly can't envision life without this machine.

Last, but not least, thanks to David Textiles, Inc., who had enough faith in me to send their wonderful line of fabrics to work with, and to Fabrics-to-Dye-For for their fabrics that are just "to die for."

# CONTENTS

CHAPTER ONE *Strips, Strata, and Curves* .................................6

CHAPTER TWO *Getting Started* ...............................10
Fabric ..................................................10
Tools and Supplies ......................................10

CHAPTER THREE *Color Makes the Quilt* ......................12
Finding a Focus .........................................15
Value ...................................................16
Transition Fabrics ......................................16
Scale ...................................................17
Background Fabrics ......................................17
Fabric Mock-ups .........................................20

CHAPTER FOUR *Creating the Strata* .........................21
Preparing the Fabric ....................................21
Cutting the Strips ......................................21
Playing with the Strips .................................22
Sewing the Strips Together ..............................24
Pressing the Strata .....................................25

CHAPTER FIVE *Creating the Templates* ......................26
The Basic Set Templates .................................26
The Basic Set II Templates ..............................30
The Advanced Set Templates ..............................32

CHAPTER SIX *Marking the Templates* ........................36
Adding the Horizontal Lines .............................39
Cutting the Templates Apart .............................37
Cutting Shapes with the Templates .......................37

# ENTS

**CHAPTER SEVEN** *Designing with Strips 'n Curves* .................... 40

   L-Shapes and Quarter Circles ........................... 40

   Creating a Focal Point ............................. 44

   Portholes and Full Circles ........................... 44

**CHAPTER EIGHT** *Piecing Techniques* ......................... 48

   Piecing ....................................... 48

   What to Do When Strips Don't Match ..................... 49

   Sewing Methods for Circles ........................... 50

   Pressing the Blocks ............................... 54

   Assembling the Quilt Top ............................ 54

   Embellishing ................................... 54

   Borders: The Next Frontier ........................... 55

**CHAPTER NINE** *Quilting Ideas* ............................ 58

**CHAPTER TEN** *More Design Possibilities* ..................... 60

   The Beg and Borrow Templates ......................... 60

   The Negative/Positive Templates ....................... 64

   Mini Strips 'n Curves Templates ....................... 65

   Flowing Ribbons Template ........................... 67

   Designing with Interlocking Circles ..................... 70

**CHAPTER ELEVEN** *Quilts to Create* ....................... 74

   Beginner Project: Citrus Flavor ....................... 74

   Intermediate Project: Colorado Sunset ................... 78

   Advanced Project: Cycloid ........................... 82

Resources ..................................... 86

Bibliography .................................. 86

Templates ..................................... 87

Index ....................................... 95

About the Author .............................. 95

# STRIPS, STRATA, AND CURVES

My friends and students whose quilts are displayed here encouraged me to write *Strips 'n Curves*. I was already hard at work writing another book, but their enthusiasm and encouragement finally gave me the courage to share this technique with other quilters.

Like most quilters, I started my quilting career with basic techniques for piecing patterns and balancing colors. As I mastered these and moved on to more complicated designs, my confidence grew and my ideas expanded. I think many quilters share this experience of expanding artistic possibilities—what starts as a craft soon becomes an art.

*Cycloid II*, 45$^1/_2$" x 37", Louisa Smith, 1998.
Made with the Basic Set templates.

I like to work with one-patch and two-patch designs, and one of my most successful experiments started when I married my favorite two-patch pattern—Drunkard's Path—with my love of strip piecing. Mesmerized by the combination of linear and circular patterns that emerged, I moved on to experiment with color, value, and texture. I was enchanted by these unexpected successes, but what hooked me on their usefulness in quilting was the fact that my beginner students had such great success with them. I think this technique is easy, fun, and habit forming. I started with the basic Drunkard's Path templates, but as I cut and pieced I saw more design possibilities emerge from the curves and strips that I assembled. Now the Basic Set includes seven templates, shown on page 8. These include the L-Shape, the Quarter Circle, the Wave, the Half Circle, the Porthole, the Full Circle, and the Square.

Skimming through these pages you'll notice that the process of making Strips 'n Curves quilts is clearly explained with drawings and photos. Most of the supplies you'll need, which are covered in the second chapter, will be familiar to you if you have used a rotary cutter. How to choose fabrics that will help you attain dramatic contrast and excitement in your quilts is covered in Color Makes the Quilt, page 12. A little knowledge of color theory is helpful, but not necessary. All you really need to get started is a great focus fabric.

Then you'll head into my "strata-sphere," where laying out, cutting strips, and sewing the strip sets together into what I call strata are covered. Creating the Strata (page 21) guides you through this process of selecting, sewing, and creating a beautiful set of strips.

A small portion of strata strips

Auditioning fabrics for a Strips 'n Curves quilt

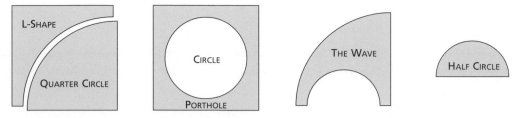

*The basic shapes for Strips 'n Curves quilts*

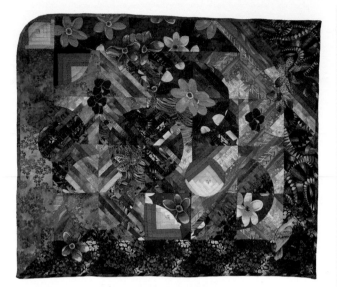

*Tropicana*, 37¹/₂" x 32", Louisa Smith, 2000.
Made with the Mini Basic Set templates.

Chapter 5, Creating the Templates (page 26), introduces you to the shapes used in the quilts, and gently leads you through the drafting process. But don't worry, plastic templates are available if you just don't want to draft anything.

Chapter 6, Marking the Templates (page 36), then takes the templates a step further by showing you how to mark them in preparation for cutting the shapes from your strata.

Marking the stripes of the strata on the templates

Then it's on to the fun part in Chapter 7, Designing with Strips 'n Curves (page 40). Circles, rings, portholes, waves…the possibilities are endless. All you need to know when designing with circles is that an L-Shape and a Quarter Circle create a block; two blocks create a Half Circle; three blocks create a Three-Quarter Circle; and four blocks create a Full Circle.

Grab your pins as you head into Chapter 8, Piecing Techniques (page 48), and you'll be ready to sew. Once you've completed your masterpiece, turn to page 58, Quilting Ideas.

Chapter 10, More Design Possibilities (page 60), encourages you to experiment with more Strips 'n Curves techniques. If you'd like some help getting started with a Strips 'n Curves quilt, try one of the projects in Chapter 11, Quilts to Create (page 74).

*Citrus Flavor* is a great beginner project, while *Colorado Sunset* and *Cycloid* were designed for the more ambitious quilter. Have fun choosing your own fabrics and getting started on your own Strips 'n Curves quilt!

*Bermuda High*, 60" x 36", Virginia Pollenz, Hampton Cove, AL, 2000. Machine quilted by Jerry Owens. Made with the Basic Set templates.

# GETTING STARTED

## FABRIC

Since I often make wallhangings, I don't usually pre-wash all my fabrics. I prewash only the fabrics that I feel will either shrink or cause bleeding problems later. You probably know the culprits: some batiks, or some of the fabrics made in India, and often the deep, rich colors such as dark teals or navies. When in doubt, check for color-fastness!

I soak the fabrics in hot water, put them in a medium-hot dryer, and iron them using spray starch. If a problem fabric bleeds a lot I use either Retayne™, which helps set colors, or Synthrapol™, which prevents migrating color from being re-deposited on the fabric. Both of these products are recommended for prewashing hand-dyed fabric.

## TOOLS AND SUPPLIES

The supplies you will need are basic to quiltmaking. Since cutting strips is a large part of my technique, you should start any cutting session with a new blade in your rotary cutter, and when you start piecing you should begin with a new needle in your sewing machine. Creating the strata (sets of strips sewn together) requires a lot of sewing, so use a good quality thread. If you fill several bobbins before you start sewing, putting together the strip sets will go faster.

If you cannot find some of the supplies listed, talk to your local quilt store. Many shop owners will order items for you.

# SUPPLY LIST

- ○ Fabrics in many color gradations

- ○ 18" gridded Collins Quilt and Sew Ruler or See-Thru Drafting Ruler

- ○ Grifhold Yardstick Compass

- ○ Gridded template plastic

- ○ Ultra fine point Sharpie® permanent markers in black, red and green

- ○ Berol® Verithin™ marking pencils in yellow and silver

- ○ Rotary cutter and cutting mat

- ○ IRIS Swiss Super-Fine $1^1/4$" pins by Gingham Square

- ○ #2 pencil

- ○ Design wall—this can be a large piece of batting or flannel-backed vinyl tablecloth tacked to a wall

- ○ Large paper for designing for advanced projects

- ○ Reducing glass or pair of binoculars

- ○ Ruby Beholder® (or value finder) (*Note: this tool does not work well with red fabric so you will need a neon-colored or green Beholder for reds*)

- ○ Reusable paper dots for numbering the strata (optional)

- ○ Sewing machine and good quality thread, 100% cotton or cotton-covered polyester

- ○ Seam ripper

- ○ Spray starch or sizing spray

- ○ Masking tape (any size)

- ○ Freezer paper

- ○ Mirrors for manipulating fabric patterns (optional)

- ○ Color wheel—optional but useful. I prefer the Color Star by Van Nostrand Reinhold

- ○ Katie's Korners Radial Rule for drafting the advanced patterns (It is helpful in drafting $1^1/2$", 3", 4", and 6" curves.) (optional)

- ○ Iron and ironing board

- ○ Quilt So Easy Discs for ease of machine quilting

(Please refer to the Resources [page 86] for information on some of the above-mentioned supplies.)

# COLOR MAKES THE QUILT

Have you ever been in awe of an antique quilt, yet on close examination realized that the workmanship was just awful? The poor quality did not matter since everyone who saw it loved the quilt for its incredible color. Color attracted you to that quilt and enchanted you. Perhaps you do not like red in general, but at a recent quilt show you were drawn to a red quilt. Sometimes it is difficult to explain such responses to color.

Color is an extremely important design element of any quilt and many books have been written on the subject (see Resources). Reading about and applying color theory can help you obtain harmony, contrast, and depth in your quilts. Using the color, texture, and patterns in your fabrics, you can create a feeling of movement and achieve special visual effects.

In my quilts I try to use a variety of large and small prints, geometrics, florals, and color-washed fabrics. In selecting fabrics I am more interested in the colors than the overall design. Today's wonderful abundance of commercial fabrics as well as the availability of many hand-dyed fabrics makes this process so much fun.

A color wheel is a great tool for learning how colors work with and against each other. It is an inexpensive tool that you can master in a short time. Color harmonies are systematic relationships on the color wheel.

An achromatic color scheme is an interesting one because only black, gray, or white are used, or any combination of the three. *Dr. Watson's Cosmos* (page 52) was created using only black, white, and tans, and is a very dramatic quilt.

Detail of *Dr. Watson's Cosmos*, page 52. Photo by David Caras

*Ripples,* 46" x 37", Cathy Granese, Stoneham, MA, 2000. Made with the Basic Set templates.

Next, look at a monochromatic color scheme that uses different tints, shades, and tones of a single hue. *Serenity* (page 46) is a good example of a monochromatic color scheme. You can achieve excellent results if you use closely graduated colors along the value scale. *Ripples* is another example of a successful monochromatic scheme. Because the strips in these quilts were constructed using closely graduated colors, your eye moves smoothly across the surface. See the strata sample on page 23.

Use your color wheel to find an analogous color scheme—three colors close to each other on the wheel. Decide on a descending order for the three colors. One color should dominate, the second color should occur less frequently, and the third color should be used to accent the others. See the strata sample on page 22.

This detail of *Reflections of Provence* is an example of an analogous color scheme.

Another popular color scheme focuses on complementary colors, which are directly across each other on the color wheel. *Rhythm of the Islands* is a perfect example. The cool blues and warm oranges in this quilt make the curves stand out, and the quilt just sings—giving it its title!

A polychromatic or multicolored scheme offers endless possibilities. Using many colors in a combination of cool and warm tones is an excellent choice for a Strips 'n Curves style quilt because the contrast between cool and warm colors is so incredible. Note how they interact in *Connections* (page 19) and *Flutterby.* See the strata sample on page 15.

*Rhythm of the Islands,* 45" square, Louisa Smith, 1998. Made with the Basic Set templates.

*Flutterby,* 55" x 45", Linda Coughlin, Franklin, MA, 2000. Made with the Basic Set templates.

# FINDING A FOCUS

The challenge of color theory is to apply it to your own fabric combinations and placements. With a little practice you will begin to understand the relationship colors have to each other. But you need more than color theory when you are standing in the middle of a quilt store trying to pull together a family of fabrics that will make your next quilt beautiful.

There are some strategies you can use to help keep your fabric shopping stress-free. If you are a beginner, start by selecting a heavily patterned focus fabric. I suggest that you pick a fabric with a lot of color and pull bolts of fabrics from the shelves that color coordinate with your focus fabric. From these, select the colors and fabrics you want for your quilt. The annual Hoffman Challenge (sponsored by Hoffman California Fabrics) is a good example of how to use a focus fabric with supporting colors.

You can also start by pulling two bolts of different colors off the shelf, such as a predominantly orange fabric paired with one that reads as blue. Then select lights and darks in each color family, looking for transition fabrics that include both colors.

*Rhythm of the Islands* focus fabric and strata choices

*Napa Valley* (page 63), *Cycloid* (page 82), *Rhythm of the Islands* (page 14), and *Nature's Splendor* (page 41) are all great examples of color schemes that started with a focus fabric.

## VALUE

Value, which refers to how light or dark a fabric appears to be, is a key player in Strips 'n Curves quilts. Collect light, medium, and dark values in each color family you plan to use in your quilt. Graduated values are used to create the curves or circles in the designs. At times you will want to use fabrics with high contrast (light with dark) or low contrast (medium with dark).

Using light and very light fabrics will help blur the edges of the circle, and enhance the illusion of a curve or rounded edge.

> **TIP**
>
> **The greater the range in value, the greater the likelihood of success. Working with several color families and collecting many values in these families promises the happiest results for both the quilt and the quilter!**

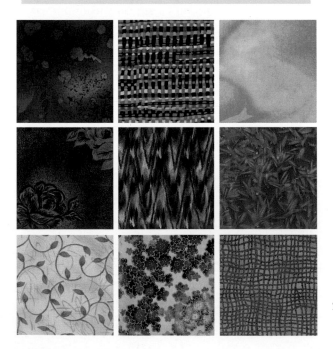

The success of *Round About*, page 30, lies in the value contrast.

Collect fabrics in any single color family that stretch from very light tints to extremely dark shades of that color. Here's a great excuse (as if a quilter ever needed an excuse) to buy lots of different fabrics. Except for the background fabric, you only need about 1/8 yard of each fabric since your strips will be cut 1 1/2" wide. Don't shy away from fat quarters, but remember that you will need to piece the strips together since I recommend you start with a strip that is at least 42" long.

Background fabrics require larger pieces; purchase half- to one-yard lengths for your background. You can also cut one to two strips from your background fabric and use them in your strata.

## TRANSITION FABRICS

Transition fabrics are used to move from one color family into another. For example, a yellow-green fabric helps make the jump from predominantly green fabrics to yellow fabrics. For a smooth transition, I prefer to place a green fabric with just a hint of yellow first, then place a green fabric with much more yellow in it and gradually make the transition from one color to the next. Books about watercolor quilts are good sources of information on the art of color transition in quilts.

Sample transition fabrics

## SCALE

Varying the scale of the print in the various fabrics you choose is another way you can add interest to your quilt. Try to use a combination of small, medium, and large prints.

A variety of print scales

## BACKGROUND FABRICS

You can cut your background shapes from strata or from a single piece of fabric. You can use just one or many background fabrics. A fabric with a splash of color or a batik works well as a single background piece, such as the L-Shapes shown below.

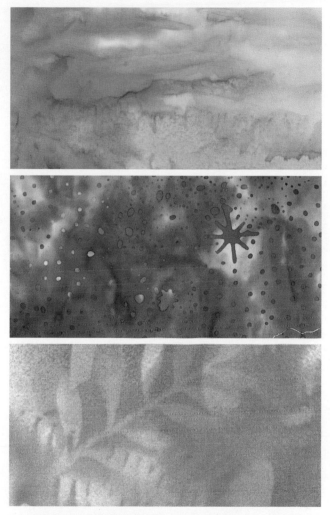

Good background fabric choices

I have two approaches for working with background fabric. The first is to make it the dominant fabric—the star player. To do this, choose a patterned fabric with many colors and use it to select all the other fabrics for your quilt. This approach was used in *Napa Valley* (page 63), *Rhythm of the Islands* (page 14), and *Nature's Splendor* (page 41). Using this color technique you can also "fussy cut" (cut out specific parts of the design) your focus fabric, as in *Napa Valley* (page 63) and *Cycloid* (page 82). Buy extra yardage since fussy cutting requires more fabric than simply strip cutting.

The second approach is to let the background fabric support the other fabrics. I often choose fairly neutral colors for the background, which leads to less contrast with the other fabrics used in the quilt. The background fabric in *Cycloid* (page 82) plays off of the softer tones of the colors in the featured Hoffman Challenge fabric.

Off-white fabrics work well as a background, and are a wiser choice than more pure whites, which tend to be intense and overpowering. Dark backgrounds—black, navy, dark purple—are dramatic and add a luminescent quality to other colors, especially to cool hues.

One last hint about background colors: Cool colors—such as blues and greens—make a better background than warmer colors—yellows or oranges. Warmer colors tend to advance, while cooler colors are just happy staying in the background as the supporting players.

Note the use of softer tones for background fabrics.

Note the choice of the predominantly green background fabric.

*Connections: a.k.a. I Can't Believe It Lies Flat,* 36" square, Kimberly White, Norfolk, MA, 1998. Made with the Basic Set templates.

After telling you to buy many fabrics, I'll risk contradicting myself by pointing out that it is possible to work with fewer fabrics. Take a look at Kimberly White's quilt *Connections: a.k.a. I Can't Believe It Lies Flat.* This quilt was designed with only fourteen fabrics in the strata and two background fabrics—one light and one dark. Because the design is symmetrical, and the fabrics range in value from light to dark, the quilt is a success.

Another example of "less is sometimes more" is my quilt, *Color Infusion* (page 55). In this quilt I used no value gradation, and relied on the contrast between the white and black strips. The success of this quilt comes from the careful placement of the strata. Negative space contrasts with positive space to emphasize the circular shapes, and the addition of the colorful geometric and floral appliqué adds a playful touch. I played with the same concept in my own version of *Connections* (page 31), where I offset the plaid strips with solid fabrics.

# FABRIC MOCK-UPS

Before I start any quilt I go through my fabric stash and pull out potential candidates, then stack them from light to dark. Then I experiment with fabrics on paper by creating a collage of the fabrics I want to use. To do this, cut a small piece of each fabric (large enough to see the color and design) and keep the clippings in some kind of order: light, medium, and dark. Then staple or glue them crazy-quilt style on a piece of white paper. This auditioning process helps fine-tune your fabric selection. It's amazing how the misfits will immediately jump out at you.

The mock-up procedure helps to reveal where you need to fill in your range of values—time to go shopping! Usually you will need more light-lights or darks since everyone seems to have plenty of mediums. Once the mock-up is complete, I slip it into a plastic protector and carry it with me. The sample card helps me stay focused when I am at the store. Once I'm home again—before I prewash my fabrics—I cut small pieces of the new fabrics and add them to my mock-up.

Fabric mock-ups for *Reflections of Provence* (page 45) and *Cycloid II* (page 6)

# Creating the Strata

The *strata* is a set of fabric strips, 1" or 1¹/2" wide, sewn together to form a new single piece of fabric. Designing with strata requires using same-size strips. After you have sewn the strata together, pieced the blocks, and finally sewn the finished blocks together, these same-size strips will line up and create the unique designs in Strips 'n Curves quilts.

## PREPARING THE FABRIC

Prewash any fabrics you think may need it, and then press all of your fabrics before you begin to cut your strips. Wrinkled fabrics lead to distorted strips so press out those wrinkles!

> **TIP**
> Using spray starch while pressing makes the cutting and piecing more accurate because it prevents stretching and distortion.

## CUTTING THE STRIPS

Cut carefully! Your results depend on precise cuts and pattern matching. If you are not familiar with rotary cutting, do some research (see Resources, page 86).

> **TIP**
> All the strips must be exactly the same width—1 ¹/2" wide for the regular size quilts and 1" wide for the smaller quilts.

When you sew the finished blocks together, the stripes created by the strips (say that five times fast!) must line up perfectly. Avoid cutting strips with a "V" or an "S" curve!

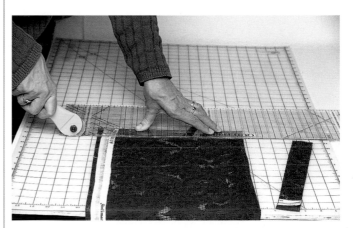

Cutting correctly

> **TIP**
> To keep your strips straight, be sure to place the horizontal lines of your ruler exactly on the fold and keep the fold near you where you can clearly see it.

A variety of textures and prints were combined in this analogous scheme that uses yellow, blue, and green.

# PLAYING WITH THE STRIPS

Before I sew my strips together I spend some time playing with them on my design wall, which can be as simple as a piece of felt or batting pinned to a wall. I lay the strips on this wall to create fabric runs that go from light to medium to dark, and then back again from dark to medium to light, and so on. Your strata should flow with value changes that create waves of color. There is no going back after you have cut your sewn strata sets using the templates, so be patient and take the time to play with your fabrics. Look carefully at the sample strata here to see the change in values.

In this polychromatic scheme all floral fabrics were used, yet waves of color were created.

*Sunset in the Japanese Garden,* 45$\frac{1}{2}$" square, Louisa Smith, 2000.
Made with the Basic Set templates.

In addition to working with gradations, you can off-set the strips as I did in *Connections* (page 31). In *Sunset in the Japanese Garden* I took this technique one step further, and worked with floral prints from Floral Wash II (a David Textiles, Inc. line of fabrics). Working with these fabrics was challenging since there were many different color families and grading the values was difficult. I played with the strips by pinning them up on the design wall. I then decided to offset them with a one-yard piece of hand-dyed fabric made for me by Fabrics-To-Dye-For.

I carefully cut the piece of fabric into strips, making sure to number the strips to keep them in the correct cutting order (I use reusable sticker dots). I then alternated these numbered hand-dyed strips with my floral strips. The result is fabulous. The eye easily flows across the composition. This technique of numbering is a must if you decide to use alternating strips and want to preserve the original design of the fabric in the completed quilt.

You can vary the number of strips that you use in your strata. A small wallhanging about 36" square will require at least 48 strips. These are all sewn together to make one complete strata. I prefer to make my strata large with many different fabrics and usually sew approximately 47 to 54 strips together. In *Connections* (page 19), Kimberly White used only two background fabrics and 14 fabrics for the strips. However, she sewed two sets of identical strata, so in fact she had 28 strips.

Sample of a monochromatic strata

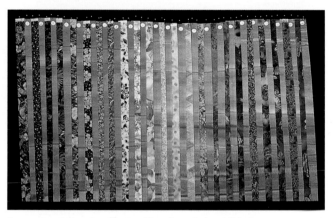

Example of florals offset with a hand-dyed fabric, carefully numbered and pinned in order

**T I P** If you have only a small number of strips make sure you make multiple sets of that strata.

**T I P** Keeping your strips pinned to the design wall keeps them organized and wrinkle-free while you sew. Another option is to arrange them in order on a folding laundry rack.

You may want to refer to the projects beginning on page 74 to get a sense of fabric amounts. When in doubt buy at least $1/4$ to $1/2$ yard of any one fabric (which yields at least four strips), and at least $1/2$ yard for the background fabric for a small wallhanging.

## SEWING THE STRIPS TOGETHER

Avoiding distortion is your main goal when sewing the strips together. Here are some tips.

**1.** Line up the top edges of the strips; don't worry about the bottom edges. Fabrics are manufactured in different lengths and can range from 42"-45" long after washing. If you have fat quarters, cut two strips and piece them together to make a strip about 42" long. Press the seam **open** (see section that follows about pressing).

**2.** A consistent seam allowance is essential and is more important than the actual size of your seam allowance. You can use the edge of your presser foot as a guide. For the sake of consistency, don't use different sewing machines for the same quilt.

**3.** Use a small stitch (about 18-20 stitches per inch). When you cut your strata, the small stitches will keep the cut ends from opening.

**4.** If your machine is equipped with a "down needle" feature, use it. It will help to keep your seam allowance more even, especially when you take a break while sewing together the long strips of the strata.

**5.** Don't tug on your strips as you sew because pulling will stretch and distort the strips. Let your machine do the work and feed the strips through evenly. Pinning is fine but shouldn't be necessary.

**6.** You can avoid curvy strips by sewing the strips together in pairs. After sewing each pair, press open the seam allowance, then place the pair back on your design wall. When all of the pairs are sewn together, sew two of those pairs together in their assigned order, then sew the groups of four together, and so on until you have joined all your strips.

**7.** Try sewing these strips in alternate directions—from top to bottom, then from bottom to top; this helps to keep the lines straight. You can still line up the tops and pin them, but then sew from the bottom up. Continue to combine pairs in order until you have sewn a complete strata. I always use this method because it is easier to keep the lines straight and the smaller units are easier to handle.

**8.** If you see that your strips are getting curvy, you can opt to make your strata with fewer strips. Sixteen strips will yield a piece big enough to cut all of the larger templates, such as the L-Shape or the Full Square. If you go this route, be sure you make more than one strata set.

**9.** Try using a walking foot (available for most machines) while sewing. These feet help feed the layers through evenly while you sew.

> **NOTE**
>
> **Because of the width of the walking foot, it may be more difficult to maintain a consistent seam allowance.**

**10.** If you have trouble sewing longer strips together, try cutting them in half (about 21"). You can also buy fat quarters or half-yard cuts and cut the strips parallel with the selvage. This definitely helps because there is very little stretch in the lengthwise grain. Keep in mind both methods will result in shorter strata—you might have to make more than one strata set.

## PRESSING THE STRATA

In quilting, seams are usually pressed to one side for strength. However, you have two options for pressing strata: press the seams in the same direction, or press the seams open.

### Pressing the Seams Open

To avoid pleating, first press the seam open on the wrong side, then flip to the right side and press again. After joining pairs of strips, bring them to the ironing board and put the tip of the iron in the seam where the pairs were joined and force the seam open.

If you prefer to sew more than two strips together at a time, and don't want to stop to press in between, you should finger-press the new seam open on the wrong side of your fabrics. I like to use a dime or other tool and do the finger-pressing on a hard surface, then go back to the ironing board and press all of the seams open on the wrong side of the fabrics. I always finish by pressing on the right side of the strata.

### Pressing the Seams to One Side

Lay your strata on the ironing board wrong side up. I like to press from the back first, then press again on the right side to make sure I don't end up with little pleats in the seams.

When you start to press, *lightly* pull on your strips and press. Don't put the tip of the iron into the seams; place it parallel to the seams. This will prevent any stretching. One way to remember to press correctly is to think of the iron as a boat, and to make sure the length of the boat is always parallel to the strips. You don't want to dive into the strips!

Once you have sewn and pressed your strata, you're halfway there! You are now ready to mark your templates with guidelines for easy placement on the strata, and then it's time to cut!

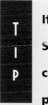

**T I P** For Strips 'n Curves quilts, open seams are preferred since they eliminate bulk and make the piecing and machine quilting much easier.

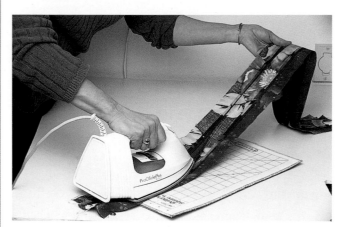

Put the point of the iron into the seams and hold the strips up while pressing—this will open the seams.

**T I P** If you are working on a miniature Strips 'n Curves quilt, remember to cut your strips only 1" wide and press all the seams to one side.

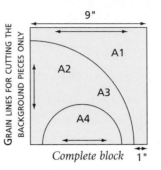

# CREATING THE TEMPLATES

The basic templates are easy and fun to work with, and will give you the piecing confidence to go on to the more intricate designs. To draft the templates, you will need gridded template plastic ($1/4$" graph). If you don't have gridded plastic you can substitute transparent (See-Thru) template plastic. It is helpful to place the template material on a gridded cutting mat while drafting the templates so your measurements are accurate.

If the thought of drafting the templates isn't appealing to you—even though I promise it's not a difficult process at all—you can purchase ready-made plastic templates (see page 86 of the Resources).

## THE BASIC SET TEMPLATES

Let's explore the seven basic templates first.

You can draft the Basic Set templates for a 9" block featured in this chapter, or you can use the block templates on page 87. The 8" and 9" blocks are the easiest and more popular sizes to use.

*Complete block*

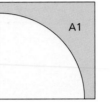

*A1: L-Shape*

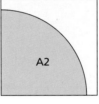

*A2: Quarter Circle*

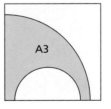

*A3: Wave*

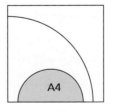

*A4: Half Circle*

*Dreamscape (The Pleiades),* 52" x 36", Amy Robertson, Walpole, MA, 1997.
Photo by David Caras. Made with the Basic Set templates.

To draft the Basic Set of templates, follow these steps:

**1.** Draw a 9" square (or 6" or 8", whatever size you desire). I use a Collins 18" gridded ruler (see Resources).

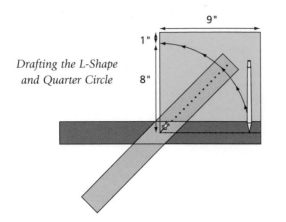

*Drafting the L-Shape and Quarter Circle*

**2.** With the aid of this gridded ruler, we are going to draw the curved shapes. The Collins ruler has small holes starting in the center of the ruler (marked from 0" to 9"). These holes are spaced every half-inch and go to one end of this ruler.

Put the zero or the end hole in the center of your ruler over a corner of the square (hold in place with a pushpin).

Put the marking pen in the hole at the 8" mark (one inch smaller than your desired block; for example, 7" for an 8" square, 8" for a 9" square, etc.) and draw the Quarter Circle, using the ruler as a compass.

Using the Collins ruler as a compass

You have now created the L-Shape (A1) and the Quarter Circle (A2) templates.

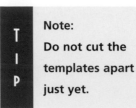

**Note:**
**Do not cut the templates apart just yet.**

**3.** For an additional shape, you can draw another half circle on the bottom of your Quarter Circle (A4).

Put the zero end of the ruler in the center of the bottom line of your Quarter Circle (4" from the left corner in a 9" template set), and put a pushpin in the hole in the center of the ruler to hold it in place.

Put your pen point in the 3" hole (for a 9" template set) away from the center point and draw a half circle. Now you have the Wave (A3) and the Half Circle (A4).

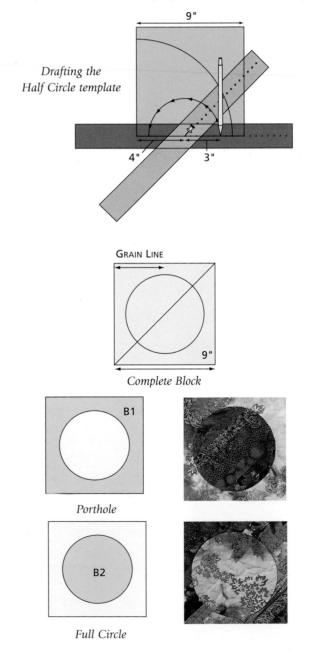

*Drafting the Half Circle template*

GRAIN LINE

*Complete Block*

*Porthole*

*Full Circle*

**4.** Draw another 9" square and draw a circle in the center, with the circle placed 1" away from the edges of the square. For instance, in a 9" square put the center point of the ruler $4^1/2$" from the edges, hold it in place with a pushpin, and put the pen point in the hole at the $3^1/2$" mark and draw a circle.

This is the Porthole (B1) and Full Circle (B2).

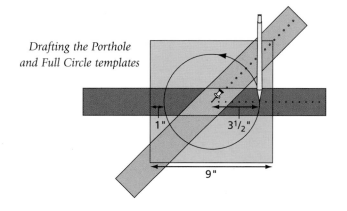

*Drafting the Porthole and Full Circle templates*

**Again, do not cut the template apart.**

Draw a line diagonally through the center of the square.

You can also use circles of different sizes, such as $4^1/2$", 5", and $6^1/2$". (See Designing with Strips 'n Curves, page 40 and Piecing Techniques, page 48.)

Once you know the drafting techniques you can be as creative as you like and come up with many, many more interesting designs. Look at the quilts in this book for inspiration. Then create your own unique designs.

*Sunset at Serengeti,* 50" square, Jodi Davila, Graham, WA, 1998. Photo by Jodi Davila. Made with the Basic Set templates.

*Fifth Rock from the Sun,* 36" square, Frances Andersen Rosenfeld, Ft. Collins, CO, 2000. From the collection of Ruth McDonald of Loveland, CO. Made with the Basic Set templates.

# THE BASIC SET II TEMPLATES

The Basic Set II is another simple design that beginners can add to their repertoire with confidence.

**1.** Follow the steps in the Basic Template Set, Steps 1-2. You now have C5 and C6.

**2.** Once you have drawn the 8" Quarter Circle in Step 2, create two more Quarter Circles, one at 3" and one at 6". This creates C, C2, C3, and C4.

**3.** Divide the 3" Quarter Circle into two halves by drawing a diagonal line through the center of your block. This helps if you want to create mirror images in your design.

*Round About,* 36" x 54", Louisa Smith, 1999.
Made with the Basic Set II templates.

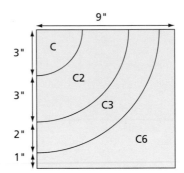

*Basic Set II block*

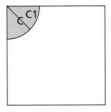

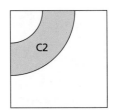

*C and C1 (C1 is half of C)*

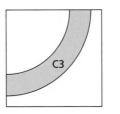

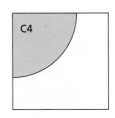

*C4 (C4=C2+C)*

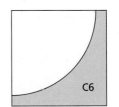

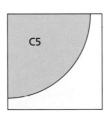

*C5 (C5=C+C2+C3 combined in one shape)*

You can combine templates to create larger circular shapes. For example, template C4 is a combination of C and C2, and template C5 is a combination of C, C2, and C3.

Using various combinations of this Basic Set II, you can turn the basic block around so the curved seams touch to create a flowing line or "trail" as in *Connections*.

Or you can just create circles as I did in *Round About*. The Basic Set II lends itself to full circles. Creating a trail can be tricky because sometimes the stripes

don't match up, but don't worry about minor matching details. In *Connections*, you can see that the mismatched stripes don't create a problem. The beauty of the Basic Set II is that mismatches occur in very few places. Once again, you can cover them with appliquéd circles (see page 48). The easiest solution is to use a stripped shape and sew it to a non-stripped or background shape as you did in the Basic Set. This way you eliminate the mismatch problem.

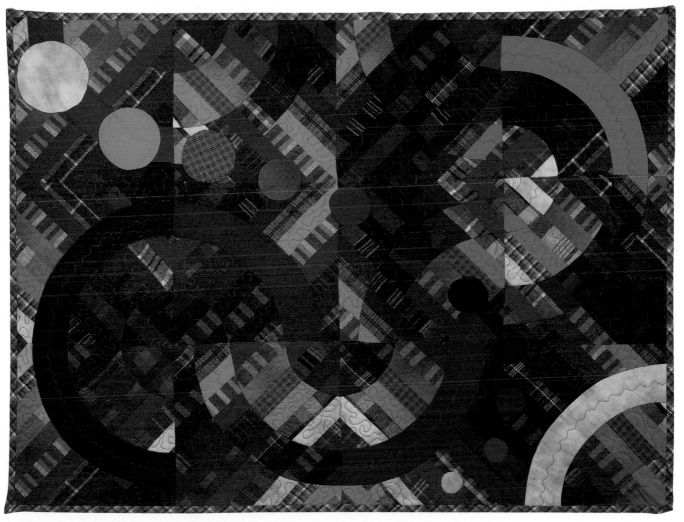

*Connections*, 36" x 26¹/₂", Louisa Smith, 1999.
Made with the Basic Set II templates.

# THE ADVANCED SET TEMPLATES

I refer to these as the "Advanced" templates because the piecing required is more intricate, and therefore recommended for advanced quilters. In the advanced set there are no extra spaces where the Quarter Circle meets the edge of the block; in the Basic Set there is 1" on each side of the L-Shape.

The Advanced Set offers more shapes that you can include in your designs. They are drafted from a different range of "starter" squares, unlike the Basic Set, which is drafted from an 8" or 9" square only. In the Advanced Set, sets are drafted from a 3" square, a 6" square, and a 9" square. The procedures for drafting are the same as for other templates. For cutting instructions see page 39.

You can create quilts using just these 3", 6", and 9" blocks. They will all work well together since they are all divisible by three.

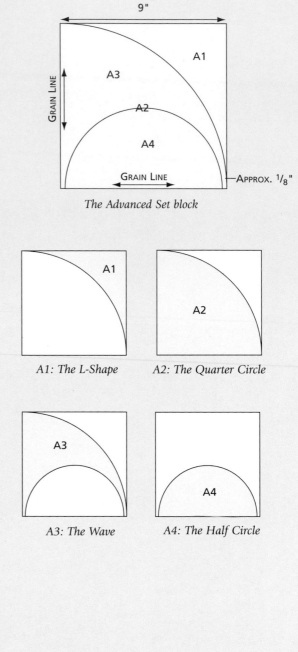

*The Advanced Set block*

*A1: The L-Shape*   *A2: The Quarter Circle*

*A3: The Wave*   *A4: The Half Circle*

*Moon Dance*, 54" x 53", Carol Wight Jones, Bonney Lake, WA, 1999.
Photo by Ken Wagner. Made with the Advanced Set templates.

You can create connector blocks that can be used to join the different-sized blocks to each other. They are the negative spaces, made up of background fabric or simply rectangles made up of leftover strata. The design possibilities are endless because you are creating with all the different sets of templates together. Remember, you are the designer. You can make these connector blocks simple—use a plain block of your background fabrics—or make them more intricate by cutting them out of your leftover strata. For examples of this procedure look at *Garam Masala* as well as *Grace.* For even more intricate designs in these negative spaces refer to the corner blocks in Project 3, page 83.

Once you are comfortable with using these sets of templates, you can move on to challenge yourself with the delightful shapes available in the template sets in More Design Possibilities, (page 60).

For now, let's move on to the next chapter, Marking the Templates. You'll learn how to mark the templates with the stripes created in the strata so they line up as you sew. Sew simple!

*Grace,* 51" x 54", Marion Connors, Weymouth, MA, 1999.
Photo by Marion Connors.
Made with the Advanced Set templates.

*Garam Masala,* 45"x 51½", Amy Robertson, Walpole, MA, 1998.
Photo by David Caras. Made with the Advanced Set templates.

# Marking the Templates

Once your strata is sewn, you are ready to mark the templates. When you cut the strata, your strips should line up perfectly and your angles must be crisp.

Marking the seam lines of your strata on your templates makes the cutting procedure much easier. The marked lines will make piecing the L-Shape and the Quarter Circle a snap. Even if your strata are perfect—all the strips evenly spaced—you have to use at least one diagonal line across the center of each of your templates. I even mark this diagonal line on the Plexiglas templates I have made (see Resources, page 86).

Before you cut your templates apart, place the template as shown at right on top of the **wrong side** of the strata. Place the center diagonal line of your template on a seam line, and trace the stitching lines to form stripes on the template. Once marked, place these lines directly on the seams of your strata on either the right or the wrong side to line them up exactly.

Marking the seam lines on your templates

---

**T I P** Working on a lightbox (which can be as simple as a piece of glass propped up over a lamp minus the shade) makes marking the templates much easier because you can clearly see the stitching lines through the plastic.

**T I P** Use a red or green Sharpie pen to mark the stripes since those colors are easier to see against most fabrics. Pull or push your strata lightly, if you have to, so your template stripes line up with the seam lines.

## CUTTING THE TEMPLATES APART

It's time to cut your templates apart! Start by cutting the L-Shape from the Quarter Circle, but leave the Porthole and Full Circle intact. Write your name on the right side of each template so you can identify the right and wrong side of the pattern. Every time you mark the back of your strata with your templates, make sure your name appears on it correctly and not in mirror image; this way you will always use your templates the same way.

> **N O T E**
>
> **If you are using the Plexiglas templates, it doesn't matter which side you use; it's the templates made of template plastic that may not be as accurate if used on different sides.**

For the Porthole and Circle, I cut a square and later appliqué the full circle onto the square as explained on page 51.

Marking the templates on your strata

## CUTTING SHAPES WITH THE TEMPLATES

When you are ready to use your templates to mark your shapes on the back of the strata, **remember to add a precise 1/4" seam allowance**. Too large a seam allowance will make the piecing impossible. I use a #2 pencil on the light-colored fabrics and a yellow or silver Berol Verithin pencil on the dark fabrics.

Cut out only a few pieces from your strata and your background fabrics. If at all possible, follow the grain markings on the templates when cutting out background pieces. However, if you are fussy cutting, as in *Napa Valley's* grape designs, page 63, you can ignore the grain lines. After you cut your background pieces, transfer the stripe markings from your template onto the seam allowance of your background fabric. These registration marks are used when you pin the stripped piece to the background piece. This procedure is similar to adding a sleeve to a garment. See page 48 for more detailed information on piecing.

Stripes marked on the seam allowance of the background fabric

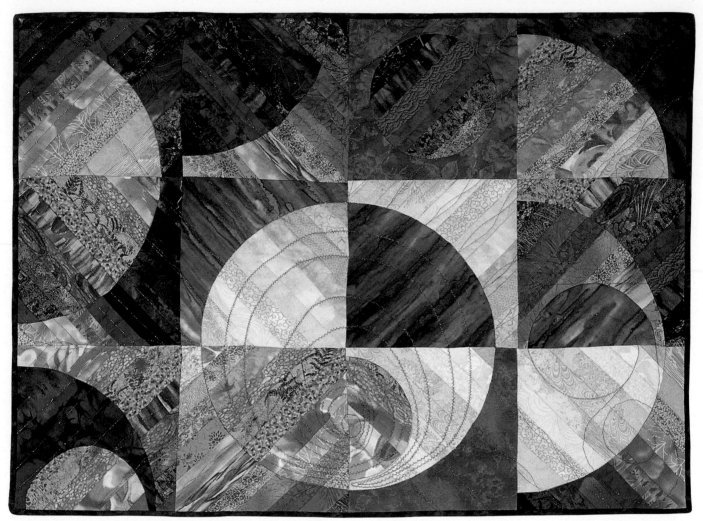

*Norwegian Sunset,* 31³/₄" x 23¹/₂", Michele Koppelman, Sharon, MA, 1998.
Notice the way the Quarter Circle is cut; the directional fabric is used diagonally
for a greater visual effect. Made with the Basic Set templates.

If you have chosen a directional background fabric, don't use the grain lines, but cut the pieces using the stripe markings from your template, and line up the directional fabric with the direction of the stripes on your templates. You will achieve a great visual effect with this method. See *Norwegian Sunset* on page 38.

Striped fabric used as a background; note the direction of the stripes.

Cutting templates with the Advanced Set is a bit trickier.

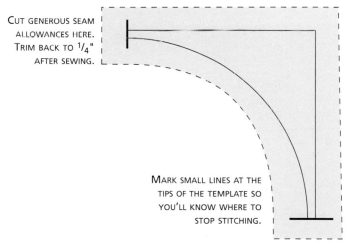

CUT GENEROUS SEAM ALLOWANCES HERE. TRIM BACK TO 1/4" AFTER SEWING.

MARK SMALL LINES AT THE TIPS OF THE TEMPLATE SO YOU'LL KNOW WHERE TO STOP STITCHING.

*Cutting procedure for the Advanced Set, template A1, the L-Shape. Follow the same procedure for template A3, the Wave.*

# ADDING THE HORIZONTAL LINES

Usually, your strips run vertical to the point of your Quarter Circle template (A2), but there may be times when you want the strips to be horizontal. Putting a piece with horizontal lines in your composition will add a point of interest. In the close-up of *Cycloid II*

notice that the strips run horizontal to the Quarter Circles in the lower left corner of the quilt (see detail below).

In order to add another set of stripes on your template you have to have already cut a Quarter Circle from your strata, otherwise it's difficult to really line up the vertical lines with the horizontal lines on your template. You should use a second color pen so you can tell the two lines apart.

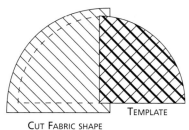

CUT FABRIC SHAPE                    TEMPLATE

*Drawing the horizontal lines on your template*

I place the fabric Quarter Circle on the table, wrong side up, then line up the Quarter Circle template with seam lines touching. The cut-out fabric shape will overlap the template for the Quarter Circle by 1/4" because of the seam allowance. Mark where the lines should meet.

Since using horizontal lines is a bit tricky, I would not recommend this method for your first piece unless you are a more advanced quilter!

Note the horizontal strips in this detail from *Cycloid II* on page 6.

# DESIGNING WITH STRIPS 'N CURVES

You don't have to have a degree in art to create a composition that is pleasing and interesting, but you do need to explore working with value. Contrast in value creates the depth and interest in the circles that are essential to the Strips 'n Curves technique. Before you begin to design a quilt, let's explore how the circles are created and used most effectively.

## L-SHAPES AND QUARTER CIRCLES

Using L-Shape and Quarter Circle templates, you can create circles of varying values. For instance, if the L-Shape is extremely light in value, and the Quarter Circle is extremely dark in value, a strong circular shape will result.

The reverse is also true. You can achieve a different effect by working with closer values. A light L-Shape set against a medium-light circle will blur the edge of the circle and make it less obvious.

A medium value used with a dark Quarter Circle will create a nice circular shape, but when the values are closer together the shapes are less obvious.

To make designs more interesting, learn to work with contrasting values. Between light and dark there are many value degrees. When cutting pieces from your strata, use value to create more or less contrast between your L-Shapes and Quarter Circles, or between your Porthole and Full Circle.

Strong contrast results in clear circular shapes.

The low contrast between the L-Shape and Quarter Circle blurs the edges of the blocks.

Even less contrast between the L-Shape and Wave

An **L-Shape** and a **Quarter Circle** create a **block**. Two blocks create a **Half Circle**, three blocks create a **Three-Quarter circle**, and four blocks create a **Full Circle**.

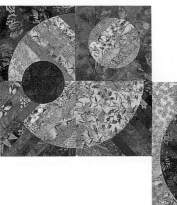
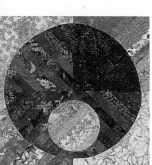

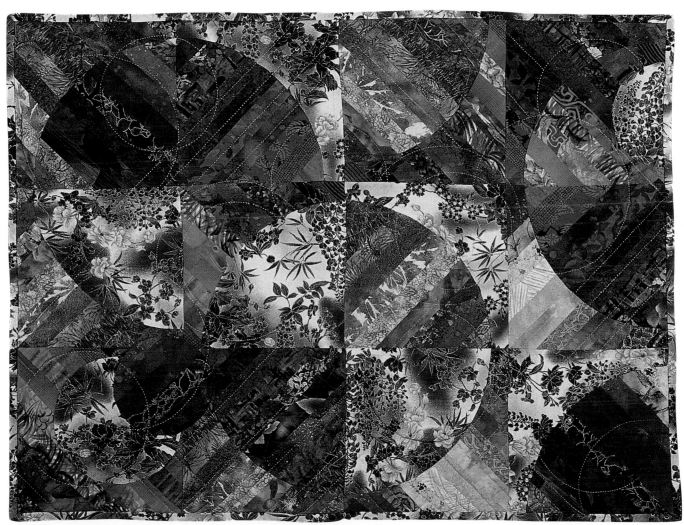

*Nature's Splendor,* 36" x 27", Paula DiMattei, East Walpole, MA, 2000.
Made with the Basic Set templates.

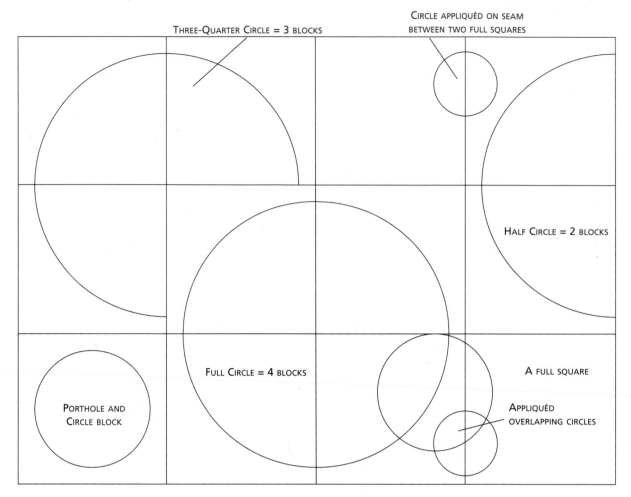

THREE-QUARTER CIRCLE = 3 BLOCKS

CIRCLE APPLIQUÉD ON SEAM
BETWEEN TWO FULL SQUARES

HALF CIRCLE = 2 BLOCKS

FULL CIRCLE = 4 BLOCKS

A FULL SQUARE

PORTHOLE AND
CIRCLE BLOCK

APPLIQUÉD
OVERLAPPING CIRCLES

*Designing with circles sample*

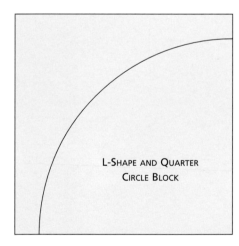

L-SHAPE AND QUARTER
CIRCLE BLOCK

**T
I
P**

**You are striving for the illusion of multiple circles within your composition. Because you want the edges of the blocks to be blurred or disappear altogether, try to get colors to flow from block to block (see page 16 of Color Makes the Quilt). If there is a strong contrast between the blocks and it is unavoidable, the addition of a Half Circle can be helpful here. In the correct value the Half Circle can be just what you need to make the transition.**

Cut a few L-Shapes, Quarter Circles, and other shapes from both strata and background and place them on the design wall. Now when you place your templates on the rest of your strata, be more selective about placement. What you cut will help create the value changes or blends that will add up to a beautiful composition. Make sure the values "flow" evenly from block to block. Your goal is to make the circles dominant and to blur the seam lines between blocks. Step back from time to time. Do you see blocks? If you do, move the pieces around more until the blocks are less obvious. Have patience, and play with these shapes until you achieve your desired effect and your composition sings.

*Sun Kissed,* 45" x 36", Louisa Smith, 2001. From the collection of Husqvarna Viking Sewing Machine, Inc., Westlake, OH. Made with the Basic Set templates.

## CREATING A FOCAL POINT

A focal point attracts attention and is most effective if placed off center, otherwise it tends to create a bull's-eye effect that is not pleasing. Your eye should move freely about the design; you want to avoid areas that stop the eye.

> **T I P**
>
> **Use loops of masking tape to stick different sized circles or appliqués anywhere on your composition when you are arranging pieces on the design wall.**

## PORTHOLES AND FULL CIRCLES

The Porthole and the Full Circle create additional interest (see *Cycloid II*, page 6). You can appliqué a 7" circle to a 9" square, or you can appliqué a circle of any size to any area of your composition (see *Fifth Rock from the Sun*, page 29). If you have an area that seems to be a problem spot, you can appliqué one or more circles on it to hide the problem and create a sense of surprise. These elements of surprise in your composition are important to the overall effect. Overlapping circles, as seen in *Reflections of Provence*, create an illusion of depth.

*Blossom*, 52" x 57", Janet Duncan Dignan, Weymouth, MA, 1999.
Photo by Janet Duncan Dignan. Effective focal points are the face and figure of a woman balanced by placing one at the left and the other toward the center. Made with the Basic Set templates.

*Reflections of Provence,* 46" square,
Louisa Smith, 1998.
Made with the Negative/Positive templates.

Use a reducing glass or binoculars to help you see the design more clearly, and discover problem areas. Strive for harmony in your composition. By working in Full Circles (four blocks together), Three-Quarter Circles, and Half Circles, you can obtain a very harmonious composition.

*Mango Sunset,* 45$\frac{1}{2}$" x 54$\frac{1}{2}$",
Carol E. Dexter, Huntsville, AL, 2001.
Photo by Carol Strong.
Made with the Basic Set templates.

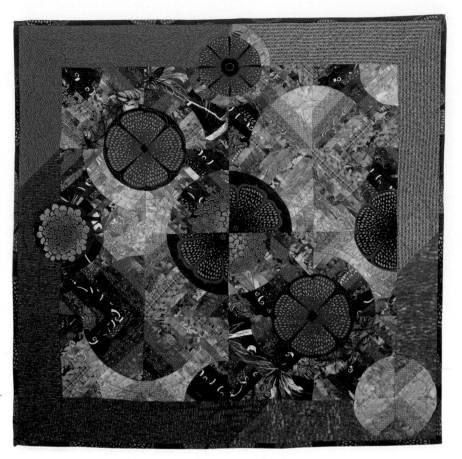

*Serenity*, 29¹/₂" square, Louisa Smith, 1998. Made with the Mini Beg and Borrow templates. See page 65 for drafting mini templates.)

Most Strips 'n Curves quilts are asymmetrical, but *Connections a.k.a. I Can't Believe It Lies Flat* (page 19) and *Serenity* are good examples of symmetrical quilts. The number of blocks you use can vary from six to thirty-six or whatever you choose.

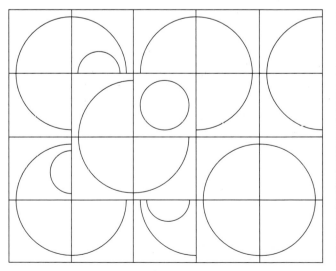

*Layout for Cycloid II*

If you are a beginner, you can create a lovely quilt with just the L-Shape and the Quarter Circle. Project 1, *Citrus Flavor* (page 74), provides you with all the tools for designing this quilt. If you are intimidated with the design process, refer to the layout of *Cycloid II*; it should also help you get started. Remember that one of the reasons I wanted to write this book is the beautiful quilts made by beginners with my Strips 'n Curves technique.

> **T I P**
>
> **Put on your favorite CD and start "playing" with the cut strata shapes on your design wall. When the CD is over, take a break, have a cup of tea, then go back to your design board with a fresh approach. It works for me!**

This auditioning is very important; step back and look at your composition. Sometimes I leave them up for a while and "live" with my composition for a period of time. Sometimes in a day or two, with a fresh approach, I will see things better and differently. That's usually all it takes.

Once you are happy with your composition you are ready to sew the blocks together.

*Un Dia en Guanacaste,* 45" x 62½", Amy Robertson, Walpole, MA, 1998. Made with the Beg and Borrow templates.

There are two methods for piecing Strips 'n Curves quilts. Hand piecing is one option, but I find machine piecing to be the easiest, provided you follow these simple steps.

**1.** Use the registration marks described on page 37 when pinning the pieces together. Then, when you piece together the strips of your L-Shape and Quarter Circle, you will have no problem aligning the seams.

**2.** Add a $1/4$" seam allowance when cutting out the shapes.

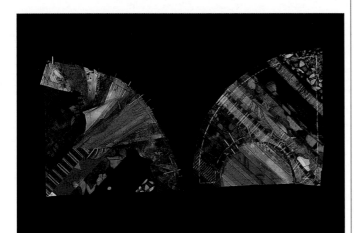

Pinning the shapes

## PIECING

The key to smooth piecing is good pinning! I use *many* pins. I pin at each connecting point and in between, every half-inch or so, as if I were sewing a sleeve to a garment. All this pinning at the seams and in between makes sewing easier and eliminates the need for a seam ripper.

When using a background piece that has no seam lines or reference points, you need to transfer the stripe markings from your template onto the seam allowance of your solid (background) piece (see photo on page 37). Then you can match the markings to the seams on the strata piece when you pin them together.

Once you have pinned all the marked points, sewing is a breeze. As you are sewing, keep turning your piece counterclockwise (or to your left) as you sew the curved seam.

> **TIP**
>
> **Always pin and sew on the full side or L-Shape side so you can control the fullness and ease it into the seam without tucks or pleats.**

*Colors of St. Lucia*, 48" square, Dennie A. Sullivan, Sun Lakes, AZ, 2000.
Made with the Basic Set templates.

**A note about pressing:** I do not do any pressing while assembling my blocks. Because pressing the circular shape can be done either toward or away from the L-Shape, I like to wait until I know what the adjacent block will be. Then I press to make sure the seams go in opposite directions to eliminate bulk. Although I recommend pressing most seams open (see page 25), in the case of the circular seams it is better to press them to one side.

Sewing the curves on the sewing machine

## WHAT TO DO WHEN STRIPS DON'T MATCH

When you start designing with Strips 'n Curves you will run into spots where the strips just do not line up. If you find that after carefully pressing the strata none of your strips measure the same width, don't fret. You can still recover. Simply cut your shapes from the strata, but don't be preoccupied with matching the strips. You will still have a wonderful piece that will look like the mismatch is intentional. I have seen this work many times.

However, if the mismatch really bothers you, you still have another option: simply combine a shape cut from the strata with a piece of background fabric. That way you eliminate the problem of matching. Sometimes mismatches are unavoidable—don't panic. If this is going to be a distracting spot, you can appliqué something, perhaps a circle, on it. See the section on Embellishing on page 54. Look at the details of quilts where the lines do not align and you will agree that the mismatch is not a big deal.

# SEWING METHODS FOR CIRCLES

Now let's tackle the Porthole and Full Circle block. If you are an experienced sewer you can piece the circle into the porthole. But as I teach I find that there are easier methods to make the block. You can use one of several methods for sewing circles onto the background square: machine appliqué, hand appliqué, or reverse appliqué. Each will use a different method of shaping and pressing the circle before applying it to the fabric. To shape the circles you can use plastic template, cardboard template, freezer paper, or Templar®.

> **T I P**
>
> **Templar is a plastic template material that can take the heat of an iron and can be used for either of these appliqué methods. Just be sure to ease the Templar out before you appliqué the circle.**

You can cover up any areas where the strips don't match exactly.

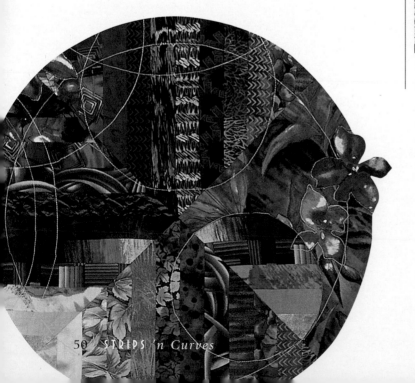

*Machine Appliqué Using a Freezer Paper Template*
Freezer paper is the best material to use for machine appliqué.

**1.** Iron a freezer paper circle the exact size you want to use onto the wrong side of the fabric, shiny side down.

**2.** Cut out the fabric shape; add a healthy $3/8$" to $1/2$" seam allowance all around the paper.

**3.** Using your sewing machine's large basting or gathering stitch, stitch all around the circle about $1/4$" from the paper's edge.

**4.** Pull up the basting thread so the fabric closes snugly around the paper; press to make the edge as crisp as possible. You can carefully remove the freezer paper now before you add the circle to the background square OR pull it out after you appliqué by cutting away the backing (see Step 6).

**5.** Center your circle on the background square, and appliqué using a blind hem stitch or narrow zigzag. The blind hem stitch stitches adjacent to the circle and every once in a while takes a side stitch or "bite" into the appliqué, securing it to the background.

**6.** If you opted to leave the freezer paper in, you can cut away the backing and pull the freezer paper out. This eliminates bulk.

There is an additional benefit to cutting away the backing: with this method you can use masking tape and tape the circle onto the background square rather than using pins.

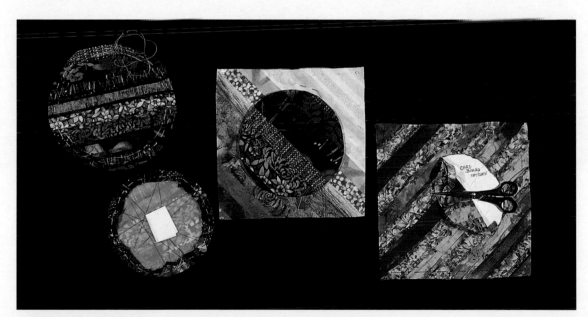

Plastic template method

*Dr. Watson's Cosmos,* 53¹/₂" x 44¹/₄", Marilyn Eimon, N. Easton, MA, 1999.
Photo by David Caras. Made with the Basic Set templates.

## Hand Appliqué Using a Cardboard or Plastic Template

This is the method I prefer; you basically follow the same steps as outlined previously. The benefit to this method is that the stripes line up perfectly every time.

**1.** Use a heavy but flexible plastic template material as a base to shape the circle.

**2.** Mark the circle on the back of your fabric and cut, adding a healthy seam allowance as in Step 2 of Machine Appliqué.

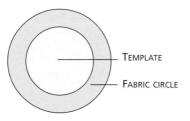

TEMPLATE

FABRIC CIRCLE

**3.** Run a basting stitch by hand or machine around the edge of the marked circle.

> **NOTE**
> When using cardboard or Templar® for these methods, the benefit is you can iron the circles with either template material inside the circle and achieve a wonderful circular shape. If you don't want to cut away the backing, you can remove the cardboard or plastic before sewing the circles to the background square.

**4.** Pull the basting thread around the edge of the plastic.

**5.** Sew from side to side across the back, like spokes on a wheel, and secure the thread.

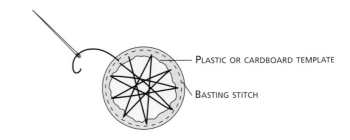

PLASTIC OR CARDBOARD TEMPLATE

BASTING STITCH

**6.** Make a loop with the masking tape and place it on the center of the back of the plastic circle, then position it on the Full Square of fabric. The masking tape will hold it in place.

**7.** Hand appliqué in place.

**8.** Cut away the back of the square about 1/2" from the appliqué stitches. Everything is removed at once: the spoke-like threads, the plastic template, and the masking tape. And you have a perfect circle!

> **TIP**
> I prefer to cut away the layer behind all my appliqué pieces since doing so reduces bulk for hand or machine quilting. I also use this method to make my quilt labels.

## PRESSING THE BLOCKS

When you are happy with your composition it's time to sew the blocks together. When my composition is pinned to the design wall I can determine the pressing direction. I prefer to alternate the direction in which I press the seams between blocks to reduce bulk at the meeting points. Press one block one way, the adjacent block the other way. Try to iron toward a background fabric for less bulk.

## ASSEMBLING THE QUILT TOP

I prefer to assemble the quilt in rows, always working with the shortest row. If my composition is four blocks by three blocks, I join three blocks together into one row, then join rows of three together to form the quilt top. When you pin the blocks to each other, the intersection between the blocks must be absolutely perfect. Working with shorter rows minimizes problems that arise when matching these intersections.

## EMBELLISHING

Embellishment can be just what your composition needs to enhance it or to cover construction problems, and it can be so much fun! We already know that there are times when strips just don't line up. For the places where this becomes a problem you can add a circle or circles, or some other shapes (see page 50). You could add an appliqué of a fabric cut-out as was done with floral shapes in *Rhythm of the Islands* (page 14). An array of circles in many different sizes, as in *Connections* (page 31), makes an interesting addition to a composition. In *Round About* (page 30), I appliquéd fifteen butterflies, some of which blended right into the quilt to blur the images. When you closely examine the quilt you are surprised to see more butterflies.

*Colors of St. Lucia* is a perfect example of how embellishment can enhance the theme of your quilt. *Tropicana* (page 8) is a thematic quilt: tropical flowers were cut out and appliquéd all over the surface. Also notice the bird appliquéd on the border in the right-hand corner. It completes the tropical theme.

Detail of *Colors of St. Lucia*, 48" square, Dennie A. Sullivan, Sun Lakes, AZ, 2000. Made with the Basic Set templates.

In *Color Infusion*, embellishment really makes the quilt! The small squares add color and interest to this piece, and the cut-out flowers make this border blend with the quilt center. You can either hand or machine appliqué these pieces. Wonder-Under™ is useful for fusing them to your quilt top before you sew the edges. Three-dimensional butterflies are effective on *Flutterby*. Two images were fused to each other with Heat-n-Bond® (which is a bit heavier than Wonder-Under). While they are still warm from pressing you can shape them any way you wish. If you don't like the shape, just iron again and remold. No sewing is necessary (except for attaching them to the quilt).

Detail from *Flutterby* (page 15)

## Quilt 'n Bead

This procedure is simply hand quilting with an occasional bead stitched in. Quilt a few stitches and add a bead. It is simple and very effective. Cathy Granese created a masterpiece using this technique in her quilt *Ripples* (page 13).

# BORDERS: THE NEXT FRONTIER

After completing a quilt I ask myself, do I need or want to add borders? Personal preference as well as an artistic evaluation determines the need for one or more borders. Let's look at some quilts in this book. *Cycloid* (page 82) and *Cycloid II* (page 6) stand alone quite well without borders. *Sunset in the Japanese Garden* (page 22) and *Reflections of Provence* (page 45) effectively use some strata in their borders, and they are beautiful. The borders in *Rhythm of the Islands* (page 14) are constructed from fabrics that weren't even used in the interior of the quilt at all.

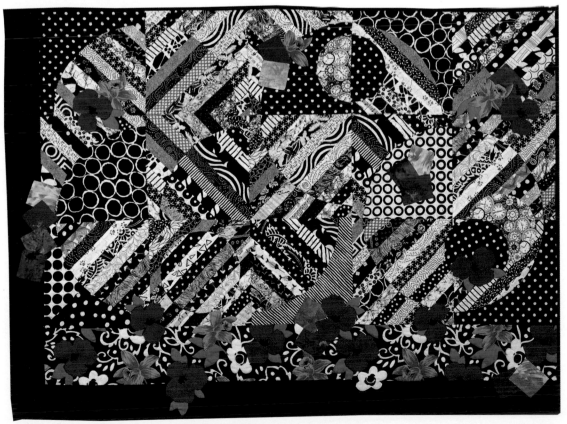

*Color Infusion*, 48" x 35", Louisa Smith, 1998. Made with the Basic Set templates.

The black and white inner borders give the eye a resting place and enhance the overall look of the quilt. You be the judge. Note that in *Stratasphere* Carol Jones very cleverly used leftover sections of strata to compose a beautiful border. She cut the strata at a 45° angle and re-pieced it to create this unusual, but interesting, border.

In another quilt by Carol Jones—*Moon Dance* (page 33)—the unusual scalloped border enhances the composition. The borders of *Reflections of Provence* (page 45) are sometimes a continuation of the quilt design. Look at the bottom left, the top right-hand corner, and the full circle created by piecing two small Quarter Circles into the border. In *Ripples*

(page 13), the predominantly red quilt has a black inner border to contain the image, yet the outside border is pieced and continues the design elements of the quilt!

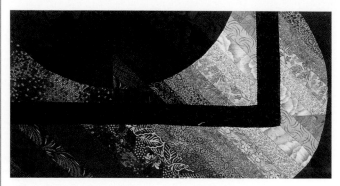

A detail of *Ripples* shows a simple but effective border treatment.

*Stratasphere*, 41¹/₂" square, Carol Wight Jones, Bonney Lake, WA, 1998. Photo by Mark Frey. Made with the Basic Set templates.

*Night Lights,* 47" x 56", Jo McCoy, Fort Collins, CO, 2001.
Made with the Basic Set templates.

Last, but not least, the simplest and most popular border treatment in my classes seems to be the use of a small inner border to contain the image followed by a slightly larger outer border of a multicolored coordinated print or prints.

Don't try to plan your border ahead of time. Wait until the quilt is finished, place it on the design wall, and stand back and ponder. Does it need borders at all? If it does, what will be the best way to go about adding them? Audition different fabrics by folding and pinning them beside your piece. Step back and let the piece talk to you. This part of the process is fun, because the end is in sight!

Smaller inner border used with a larger outer border

Whether you are quilting by hand or by machine, quilting stitches add texture, movement, and interest to your composition. Some quilters prefer large meandering machine quilting lines as seen in *Color Infusion* (page 55) and in the detail of *The Wise Woman Quilt*. As you can see, this can be very successful. For a more linear effect you can quilt in the middle of the strips. In *Colorado Sunset* (page 78), this turned out to be the perfect solution. This method of quilting in the middle of the strips—by hand or machine—is the easiest way out; you don't have to deal with a lot of seam allowances.

Detail of *Sun Kissed,* page 43

*Moongazing,* 36" square, Cathy Clay, Sharon, MA, 1998.
Photo by David Caras. Note the quilting in the middle of the strips.
Made with the Basic Set templates.

Another popular method is to create circles in a variety of sizes. Get out every saucer, bowl, or platter in your kitchen cupboard and use them to make cardboard template circles. Trace these randomly on your top, then quilt them.

A combination of the last two methods, the circles and the quilting in the center of the strips, was done in *Cycloid II* (page 6). I received an honorable mention for the quilting design in this quilt. Imagine that! It was so simple! Sometimes simplicity is the best solution.

In *Reflections of Provence* (page 45), I again simply followed some of the design elements in the quilt and enhanced the rest with—what else? Circles! And, of course, quilting in between the strips. Hey, it works for me. My message is that you should not agonize over the quilting. The dynamic designs in the quilt will tell you what and where to quilt. Simplicity is the key. I have yet to see an ugly Strips 'n Curves quilt, and I have been making them and teaching the process for years! From beginner to advanced, all are a pleasure to view, and isn't that why we make quilts?

If you prefer to machine quilt, check out the different quilting designs used in *Citrus Flavor* (page 74) and *Sun Kissed* (page 43). If your machine is equipped with different stitches, you can create a lot of interest with these stitches in the middle of your strips. Then you can switch to free-motion quilting for the larger background areas. It's fast and fun! The continuous star design used in Carol Jones's *Moon Dance* (page 33) is shown below. It can be either hand or machine quilted.

Note the different stitches and free-motion quilting in this detail from *Citrus Flavor* (page 74).

Detail from *Wise Woman Quilt* by Mel Tuck, Springfield, VT.

# More Design Possibilities

Once you have mastered a basic Strips 'n Curves quilt, you may want to explore other template sets. The best thing about the Strips 'n Curves technique is the endless design possibilities that can be created with the different template sets in this book. You could easily design an entire series of quilts by creating variations on a theme, which I encourage you to try! In fact, working in a series will give you the opportunity to create original designs. I have found this style of quilting is habit forming—one quilt leads to another.

Keep in mind that the Strips 'n Curves technique can be used to create a bed-size quilt. Try using the Basic Set II and the Beg and Borrow set in a 12" block size and add more blocks and rows to the quilt design.

Let's explore some of these designs, starting with the Beg and Borrow templates.

## THE BEG AND BORROW TEMPLATES

The templates in this set can be used either by themselves or by using part of another template, hence the name Beg and Borrow. I have worked with 9" blocks and 12" blocks. The Quarter Circle can be divided into three templates. But in this case the small Quarter Circle template, A4, can also be divided into two equal pieces—A7. These templates—A4 and A7—are used for mirror-image piecing and fussy cutting.

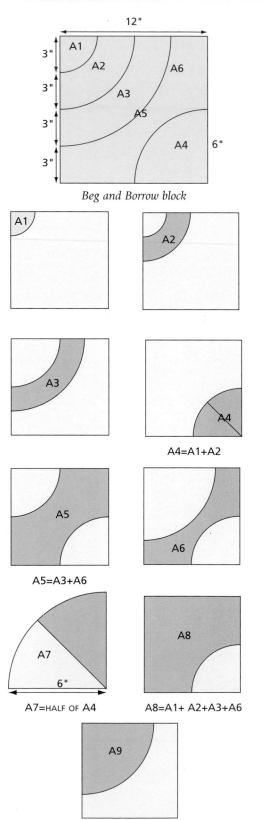

Beg and Borrow block

A4=A1+A2

A5=A3+A6

A7=HALF OF A4     A8=A1+ A2+A3+A6

A9=A1+A2+A3

Now that you are somewhat familiar with creating the templates, these should be a snap.

**1.** Start with a 9" or 12" square, and make the circular shape as we did in the Basic Set of templates (see page 28). Make an arc at the 3" point (A1) and another arc at the 6" point (A2). For the 12" block you would also make an arc at the 9" point (A3).

**2.** To create A4, draw an arc diagonally across from A3 at the 3" point (which would be the 6" point for the 12" block).

**3.** That's all the drafting you need to do! Now all you need to do is trace your drafted block onto the plastic template material to create templates A1–A9.

*Donna's Blue Galaxy,* 76" x 86", Mary L. Penton, Huntsville, AL, 2000.
Strips 'n Curves make great bed-sized quilts! Made with the 12" Basic Set II templates.

There are many options for using the shapes alone or in combination, which can all be cut from either the strata or the background fabric.

*Arco Iris* and *Summer Rain* are beautiful examples of quilts made with the Beg and Borrow set templates.

Detail of *Summer Rain,* Marion E. Connors, Whitman, MA, 2000. Made with the Beg and Borrow templates.

*Arco Iris,* 53" x 63", Amy Robertson, Walpole, MA, 1991. Photo by David Caras. Made with the Beg and Borrow templates.

*Napa Valley* illustrates the different ways these templates can be used to maximize the beauty of a feature fabric, in this case the grapevine print. The $4^{1}/2$" set of template patterns are on pages 90-91. Play with them to see how you, too, can use these templates to get the best features out of your fabric.

This is by far the most versatile of template sets. They require more piecing, but they also offer more design possibilities.

The 9" and 12" block templates are a good size to work with, but the mini or smaller version of this template set (*Serenity,* page 46) is a favorite among my students.

*Napa Valley,* 36" square, Louisa Smith, 1997.
Made with the Beg and Borrow templates.

# THE NEGATIVE/POSITIVE TEMPLATES

Light and dark contrast, as discussed earlier, is even more relevant in these compositions since the lights and darks create new patterns and add depth to these designs. The piecing for this set of templates is not any more difficult than for the Basic Set II, so give it a try.

Creating the Negative/Positive templates is not difficult. Use the templates on page 91, or you can follow these simple steps to draft your own.

**1.** Start with a 9" square, and create an arc at the $4^1/2$" point (A), and create a second arc across from it at the same point (E).

**2.** Create a third arc on this side at the $3^1/2$" point (D).

**3.** Draw a diagonal line from corner to corner.

**4.** You can draw a second diagonal line that divides A in half to create template A1.

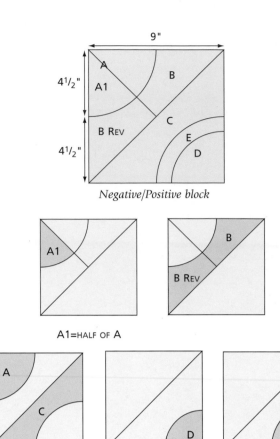

*Negative/Positive block*

A1=HALF OF A

A=D + E

*Layout using the Negative/Positive templates*

*Key Lime Pie,* 56$\frac{1}{2}$" square, Carol Wight Jones, Bonney Lake, WA, 2000.
Made with the Negative/Positive templates.

Take a moment to review the quilt layout using these templates. Make several photocopies of this layout. Using a pencil, start to shade the positive areas and leave the negative areas blank—as if it were a black and white quilt. Keep changing these areas and you will end up with many wonderful designs. You can use some or all of the templates. You could make a wonderful composition with just templates A and C; don't count this one out—it can be as simple or complicated as you wish to make it.

Another good exercise is to make several copies of the larger blocks, then cut them apart and play with the pieces. This way you can position and reposition them to make your own designs or trails. And eventually you can shade in the areas to see your design possibilities in advance. When you cut pieces out of your strata and start playing on your design wall with this Negative/Positive template set, you will be amazed at the possibilities. I think this design has the most potential for making complex and interest-ing quilts. For inspiration you may want to review the quilts *Reflections of Provence* (page 45) and *Key Lime Pie.*

## MINI STRIPS 'N CURVES TEMPLATES

This set of templates is a smaller version of the Basic Set templates.

The small quilt on page 66 was designed for the Miniature Celebrity Quilt Auction at the International Quilt Festival in Houston (1997). To draft this mini set, simply refer to the Basic Set templates or any other template set you may desire, but start with a 5" or 6" square.

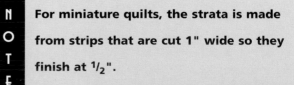

**N O T E** **For miniature quilts, the strata is made from strips that are cut 1" wide so they finish at $\frac{1}{2}$".**

Another important point about this mini set is the pressing. It is virtually impossible to press the seams open because they are so narrow. Press all the seams in one direction. I hand quilted this piece and had no problems, but I used a thin quilt batting to minimize bulk.

For added interest I cut some of the Quarter Circles and L-Shapes out of pieced Log Cabins (also constructed using 1"-wide strips). Take a moment to look at the photographs of *Aurora* and *Tropicana* (page 8) to see how these interesting Log Cabin pieces are cut and pieced into the quilt.

*Aurora,* 20" square, Louisa Smith, 1997.
Made with the Mini Basic Set templates.

In *Serenity* (page 46), *Hawaiian Holiday*, and *Hawaiian Holiday II* you can see there is no need to go through all the trouble of cutting up a Log Cabin piece. You can make them simply and effectively by using the Beg and Borrow Set with basic strata and perhaps a little fussy cutting. Notice also that *Serenity* is monochromatic and symmetrical.

## FLOWING RIBBONS TEMPLATE

Flowing Ribbons was created when I experimented with another curved one-patch—the clamshell. The Flowing Ribbons design is nothing more than two half-clamshells combined. This simple one-patch template saves time and energy. It is also great for playing with a lot of color. Because of the intricate piecing, I recommend this one for the more experienced quilter.

If you take a look at one of the project quilts, *Colorado Sunset* (page 78), as well as *Purple Haze* (page 68), you will notice that twisting the Flowing Ribbons block in a new direction resulted in two different looks.

*Hawaiian Holiday*, 18" square, Louisa Smith, 2000. Made with 1"-wide strips and smaller strata and blocks.

*Hawaiian Holiday II*, 30" x 24", Louisa Smith, 2000. Made with the Mini Beg and Borrow templates.

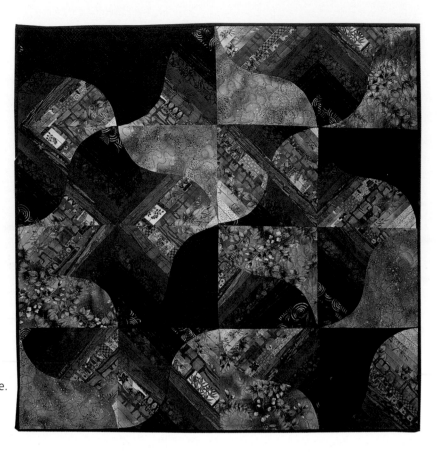

*Purple Haze,* 32" square, Vicki Carlson,
Fort Collins, CO, 2000.
Made with the Flowing Ribbons template.

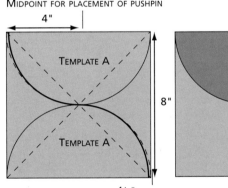

MIDPOINT FOR PLACEMENT OF PUSHPIN

4"

TEMPLATE A

8"

TEMPLATE A

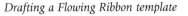

AT LEAST 1/8" FROM
EDGE OF BLOCK

*Drafting a Flowing Ribbon template*

**NOTE**

**This template cannot be reversed. Write your name on the template so when you accidentally reverse it, you know to turn it the correct way. Two reversed pieces can be sewn together in the same block, but you can't combine a reversed and a non-reversed piece in the same block.**

**1.** Begin with an 8" square of gridded template plastic.

**2.** Draw two diagonal lines from corner to corner.

**3.** Using the 18" Collins Quilt and Sew ruler, find the midpoint at 4" on any side. Insert a pushpin through the 0 hole on the ruler into the 4" mark on your gridded plastic, and draw a half circle. It goes right through the center of your 8" square.

**4.** Repeat Step 3 to create another half circle on the opposite side of the square.

**5.** The half circles touch the edges of your 8" square. In order to make the piecing and cutting easier, you need to move one edge of the half circle in approximately 1/8" from the edge of the template.

The dark line in the illustration shows how to adjust the curved line 1/8" in from the edge in the upper left and lower right corners of the square to create template A.

## Piecing for Flowing Ribbons

As you can see, there are **two curves** in this template. The diagonal line of your template marks the halfway point. You can refer to the regular piecing technique of pinning the curve, but this pattern needs to be done in two steps. And since I always prefer to sew with the fuller side on top, I pin only one curve (to the halfway point or midpoint), and stitch it. In other words, stitch to the middle of the block, then turn it over. The fuller side is again on the top; again pin the seam, sew the second curve, and your block is complete.

The two-step piecing technique for Flowing Ribbons

The ribbons can be created in strata that varies from a very light to a very dark, so the different values flow like ribbons diagonally across the surface of your quilt. For instance, the very light strata creates a light-colored ribbon and the very dark creates a dark ribbon next to the very light one. Or you can play with color and have strata in various colors so that a yellow strata, a blue strata, and a green strata create different color ribbons.

*Colorado Sunset,* Project 2 on page 78, offers another version of this set. In this quilt the blocks are turned. My friends nicknamed this *Puzzle Pieces.* Have fun creating by manipulating this template. Turn and twist it on purpose, but just remember to piece it to a similar shape. Enjoy.

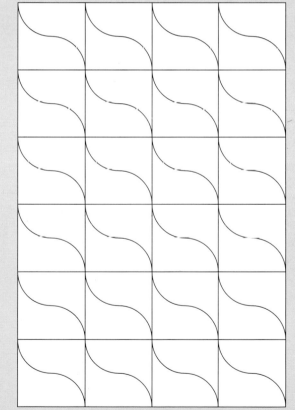

*Layout using the Flowing Ribbons template*

# DESIGNING WITH INTERLOCKING CIRCLES

In this design you will be working with both the 1" (cut $1^1/2$") and the $^1/2$" (cut 1") strips to create your strata. But the designing part is more freeform—no templates to draft! We will work with freezer paper and your design.

To start you will need large design paper; I use paper designed for easels. Any office supply store carries this large block of paper with a one-inch grid, which is very helpful in the design process. The standard size is 27" by 34". You can either use this size or you can tape two pieces side by side. You can also look for paper commonly used for making clothing patterns that has been gridded with dots, which will aid

you in the design process as well. Using the Collins 18" gridded ruler, start drawing a very large circle (any size you desire) anywhere on your design surface. I added more little holes to my ruler so I can create larger-size circles. The Grifhold Yardstick Compass is a wonderful tool for drawing large circles (see Resources on page 86).

> **T I P**
>
> **You can use a pushpin to create more holes in your ruler—just push and twist the pushpin into the plastic of your gridded ruler.**

*Chop Sticks*, $51^1/2$" x 32", Louisa Smith, 2000.
Made with the Interlocking Circles design.

*Quilt assembly diagram for* Chop Sticks

Once you have a large circle on your graph paper (and part of this circle could easily be drawn to go off the edge of your paper), draw at least two more circles. I usually ask my students to draw three different-sized circles onto the paper; they should overlap in some areas, and one or more circles should travel off the edge of your paper. A diagram of *Chop Sticks* is shown above.

Once you have drawn three (or more!) circles, you should draw horizontal, vertical, and diagonal lines to create a pleasing design. These lines can cut right through your circles. You will be using your pencil and eraser quite a bit; just loosen up and have some fun. I suggest drawing lots of lines and then erasing parts of those lines. It sounds complicated, but just get started. It will become self-explanatory and quite easy.

When you are relatively happy with your design, you can add lines either 1" or $1/2$" apart to show the placement of your strata. Take another moment to look at the quilt photo. Notice you can place your strata horizontally, vertically, or even diagonally. I like to use a #2 pencil so that it will erase easily, but once I have completed my design I like to go over the lines with a thick black marker so I can see the lines from the back.

When you have completed your entire design, turn the paper over and copy (from the back) the different templates you will need onto freezer paper with a big black marker. Make sure you add registration marks on the curved seams so you can pin them to each other as you did in the Basic template set. You should always add these marks to make sure the concave and the convex seams match up where they should. Cut the templates apart and iron them shiny side down onto the back of your fabric or strata. Then mark around the freezer paper templates with pencil—this will be your sewing line. Add seam allowances as you cut the shapes out.

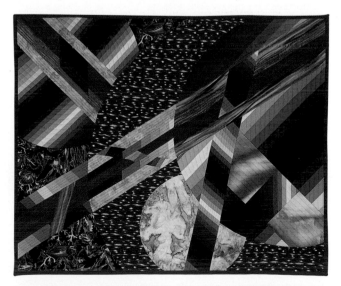

*Looking Thru the Stratasphere*, 32" x 27", ©Gwyned Trefethen, Sherborn, MA, 2000.
Made with the Interlocking Circles design.

Now you are ready to piece! This is a liberated version of Strips 'n Curves and a class favorite. It is an easier and faster method, and we know that simpler is usually better. Give it a try and have fun. Remember in this design anything goes. I had so much fun with this technique that I made another quilt from the same design; see *Winner's Circle*.

I hope that the patterns mentioned give you plenty of inspiration to make many, many quilts, and that you will be able to create patterns of your own using this simple technique. This definitely calls for a series of quilts—most likely, many series of quilts. Keep me posted. I would love to hear from you.

**T I P**

I prefer to iron my freezer paper templates to the back of my strata and fabric and draw a pencil line all around the freezer paper, then pull it off. Then I cut it out with a $\frac{1}{4}$" seam allowance and use the pencil lines to pin and sew the pieces together.

*Winner's Circle*, 52" x 33", Louisa Smith, 2000.
Made with the Interlocking Circles design.

*Drifting Apart*, 31³/₄" x 23¹/₂", Michele Koppelman, Sharon, MA, 2000.
Made with the Interlocking Circles design.

*Citrus Flavor*, 32" x 40", Louisa Smith, 2000.
Made with the Basic Set templates.

# Citrus Flavor

**QUILT SIZE:** 32" x 40"

**SKILL LEVEL:** Beginner

This quilt is a perfect beginner piece. It's a confidence builder because almost every piece is constructed out of a stripped piece and a background piece. There are only a few places where you actually have to line up the strips and there is also a part where the strips **don't** line up and you may add some kind of embellishment! Take a moment to study this quilt before selecting your fabrics.

## FABRIC TIPS

An easy way to approach shopping for your first Strips 'n Curves quilt is to find a fabric that you absolutely love that features a variety of colors. As you can see from the photo, the focus for this quilt was a wonderful print with green, yellows, and oranges. I chose strips that ranged from greens, to yellow-green, to yellow, to yellow-orange, and orange. Let the focus fabric be your guide; pull fabrics off the shelves until you have a pleasing array, **then** put them in the correct value order.

I selected about 20 fabrics that coordinated with the focus fabric, then put them in value order until I had about 17 fabrics (this number can include your focus fabric). I left out the few fabrics that refused to play well with the other fabrics.

**Please note:** The first and last strip of your strata are not as visible in your design, so they are not as important; this may help you in making your fabric selections.

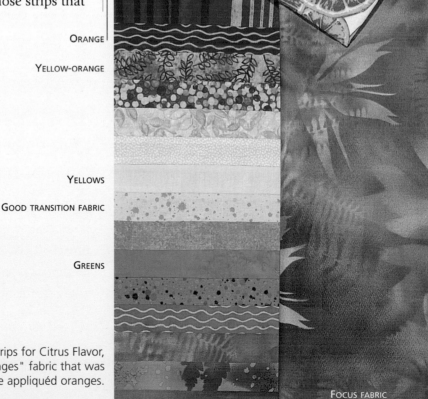

ORANGES FABRIC FOR APPLIQUÉ

ORANGE

YELLOW-ORANGE

YELLOWS

GOOD TRANSITION FABRIC

GREENS

FOCUS FABRIC

Focus fabric and strips for Citrus Flavor, with the "oranges" fabric that was used for the appliquéd oranges.

## FABRIC REQUIREMENTS

$1^1/2$ yards of a focus fabric—a multicolored print

$1/4$ yard each of 17 different fabrics that coordinate with your focus fabric, ranging from light to dark. You may include your focus fabric in your strata; in that case you only need to choose 16 other fabrics, but add $1/4$ yard to your focus fabric yardage.

$1^1/2$ yards for the backing and sleeve

Batting: 36" x 44"

## ASSEMBLY INSTRUCTIONS

**1.** Enlarge the 8" Basic Set templates (on page 87), then trace onto template plastic using a permanent marking pen. Templates for this project include the L-Shape, the Quarter Circle, and the Full Square.

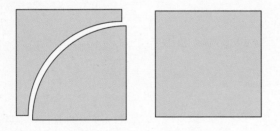

I make my templates **without** the seam allowances added because I prefer to sew exactly on the marked lines. However, my students often prefer to include the $1/4$" seam allowances on their templates.

**2.** Cut four $1^1/2$"-wide strips of **each** of your 17 fabrics.

**3.** To make your strata, sew the 17 strips to each other, arranging your strips in waves of color, dark to light, light to dark, etc. Refer to the sewing tips on page 24. Use a small stitch since you will cut these strip sets later and do

not want them to come apart. Repeat this procedure four times so you end up with four complete strata sets. This way you handle only 17 strips and you will build your confidence to tackle larger strata for other projects.

**4.** Press the seams open as instructed on page 25. Spray starch the whole set, giving it a final pressing on the right side before cutting your shapes.

**5.** Mark the stripes created by the seams of the strata on your template following the instructions on page 36.

**6.** Now you are now ready to cut your shapes out of the strata sets. Refer to the quilt diagram to make sure you are cutting the correct pieces; you will notice that you either cut pieces from your strata (stripped fabric) or the focus fabric. Move your template all over your strata so you can cut as many different colors as possible.

Here's a breakdown of what you will need to cut:

L-Shape from focus fabric: Cut 10.

L-Shape from strata: Cut 8.

Quarter Circle from focus fabric: Cut 8.

Quarter Circle from strata: Cut 10.

Square of focus fabric: Cut 1.

Square from strata: Cut 1.

**7.** Refer to page 48 to piece the blocks. Pin them exactly on the marked lines using silk pins, and sew on the sewing machine or by hand. (As noted before, you can line up the edges carefully if you have included the seam allowances in your templates.)

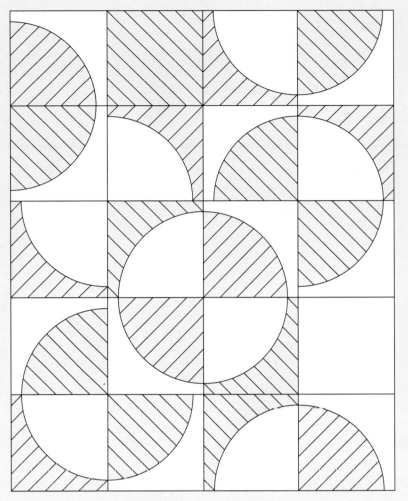

*Quilt assembly diagram for* Citrus Flavor

**8.** Arrange the blocks according to the assembly diagram, then sew them into five rows of four blocks each. Press the seams open. Follow the same pressing procedure: press from the back, then from the front.

**9.** Join the five rows to each other to complete the quilt top.

**10.** Press carefully. If there are points where the strips don't line up you can appliqué a circle or other embellishment.

**11.** Layer the top, batting, and backing and baste layers together.

**12.** Refer to page 58 for some quilting ideas. If you want to quilt by hand just remember there are a lot of seams in this piece, so keep your quilting designs as simple as possible.

**13.** Bind with your focus fabric. Add a hanging sleeve, and a label with your name, date of completion, and any other information you might want to add.

Give yourself a pat on the back (or eat some chocolate, or dance, or...). Welcome to the world of Strips 'n Curves! That wasn't hard at all, and now you are ready to try your hand at Project 2: *Colorado Sunset.*

***C****olorado Sunset*, 32" square, Louisa Smith, 2000.
Made with the Flowing Ribbons template.

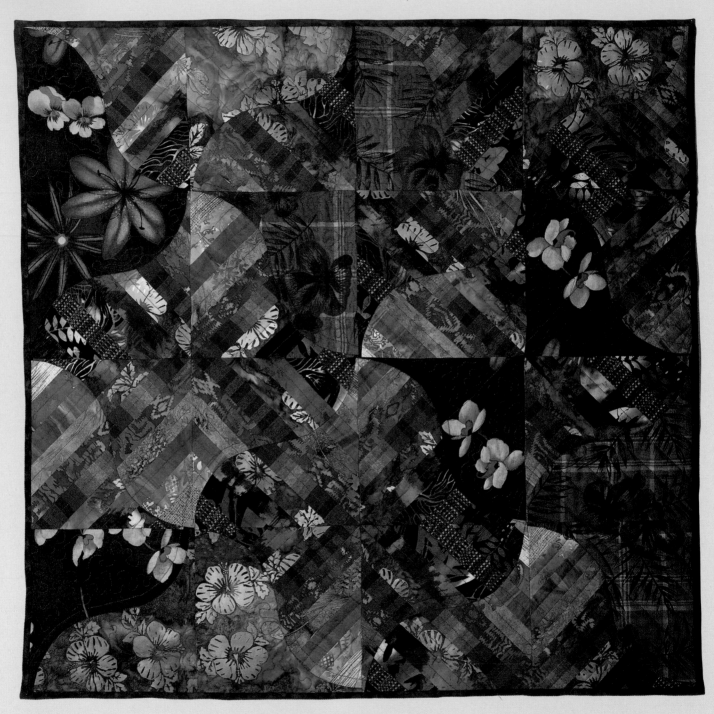

# Colorado Sunset

QUILT SIZE: 32" square

SKILL LEVEL: Intermediate

This quilt is made following a fairly easy procedure. The difficulty lies in the fact that there are two curves in each seam. The curve is not any more difficult to handle than the Basic Set with the exception of having to do it twice. The whole block consists of only two pieces—one template, two steps. Try it, you'll like it.

## FABRIC TIPS

For this project, first choose 3 color-coordinated fabrics. One will act as your focus fabric, and the other two are supporting players for the focus fabric. One can be dark, one medium, and one medium-light. They are companions, and that's all they need to be. In this case the companions are about the same value.

Then bounce off of the first 3 fabrics and find 14 other fabrics ranging from lights to darks to end up with a total of 17 different fabrics. In this quilt, many of the multicolored fabrics ended up as great transition fabrics because they shared similar colors.

> **TIP**
>
> In selecting fabrics, find a focus fabric, then select any or all fabrics that you feel coordinate, then arrange them by value from lightest to darkest. Eliminate any fabrics that just don't work and keep the ones that help make a transition from one fabric to the next.

FOCUS FABRIC          COMPANION FABRICS

Fabrics selected for *Colorado Sunset*

## FABRIC REQUIREMENTS

1 yard focus fabric

$1/2$ yard each of 2 other fabrics as noted in Fabric Tips

$1/4$ yard each of 17 fabrics

$1^{1}/4$ yards for the backing and sleeve

Batting: 34" square

## ASSEMBLY INSTRUCTIONS

**1.** Enlarge the 8" Flowing Ribbons template (on page 92), then trace onto template plastic using a permanent marking pen. ($1/4$" seam allowances can be added; see Project 1.)

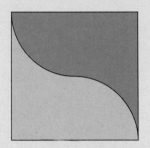

*The Flowing Ribbons design is made using just one template.*

**2.** Cut four $1^{1}/2$"-wide strips from each of the 17 fabrics.

**3.** To create your strata, sew the 17 strips to each other, starting with the lightest strip and ending with the darkest strip. Use a small stitch since you will cut into these strip sets later and do not want them to come apart. Repeat this procedure to make a total of four strata sets.

**4.** Press the seams open as instructed on page 25. Spray starch the whole set, giving it a final pressing before cutting out your shapes.

**5.** Mark the stripes created by the seams of the strata on your template following the instructions on page 36.

**6.** You are now ready to cut your shapes from your strata. Mark around the template with a marking pencil. If you did not add the seam allowances to your template, remember to add $1/4$" seam allowances as you cut out the Flowing Ribbons shapes. The marked lines on your template make it easy to line it up with your strips.

**7.** Refer to the quilt assembly diagram to make sure you are cutting the correct pieces. You either cut pieces from your focus fabric, the secondary fabrics, or from the strata.

Each Flowing Ribbons block consists of two pieces. In *Colorado Sunset* the template is used without mirror images, so there is no need to reverse the template.

Here's a suggested breakdown of what you will need to cut:

19 from your strata

5 from your primary focus fabric (in *Colorado Sunset* the purple with the bright flowers)

4 from your second focus fabric (in *Colorado Sunset* the plaid floral)

4 from your third focus fabric (in *Colorado Sunset* the floral batik)

You can cut as many or as few of the 3 main fabrics as you like; you are encouraged to create your own design.

*Quilt assembly diagram for* Colorado Sunset

**8.** To prepare the blocks for piecing, first pin the curves carefully, exactly on the marked lines with silk pins. This is a two-step sewing technique (see page 69). Keep the concave side on top and sew on the machine or by hand if preferred. (If you added the seam allowance to your template line up the edges carefully.)

**9.** Complete all the blocks, then sew the blocks into 4 rows.

**10.** Press the seams open. Press from the back first, then from the front.

**11.** Join the 4 rows together to complete the quilt top.

**12.** Layer the top, batting, and backing and baste the layers together.

**13.** You can machine quilt a large meandering stitch all over the piece or stitch in the middle of your strips. Or you can follow the curves created by the pattern. Because the quilt top is busy and graphic, it does not need extra quilting designs to enhance the overall look of the piece. If you want to quilt by hand remember to keep the designs simple because there are so many seams.

**14.** Bind with your focus fabric.

*Cycloid*, 36" square, Louisa Smith, 2000.
Made with the Advanced Set templates.

# Cycloid

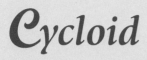

QUILT SIZE: 36" square

SKILL LEVEL: Advanced

This quilt is created with the Advanced Set templates, so the piecing is a bit more intricate. The templates used in this symmetrical piece include the Quarter Circle, the L-Shape in various sizes to 9", and elongated to a 6" x 9" and 6" x 12" rectangle, and an occasional Half Circle for additional interest. Cutting all the shapes in your choice of fabric or strata will make this experience fun and will build confidence in your own designing abilities.

## FABRIC TIPS

For this quilt you will again want to choose a focus fabric—in this quilt it's a multicolored floral. Then select as many coordinating fabrics as you can find—the more the merrier! About 27 fabrics were used in this strata, and there are many background fabrics (see Fabric Requirements). In *Cycloid* we did some "fussy" cutting, so the floral fabric lends itself well to this procedure. Try to select fabrics ranging in value from very light to very dark. Choose your backgrounds **after** selections have been made for the strips.

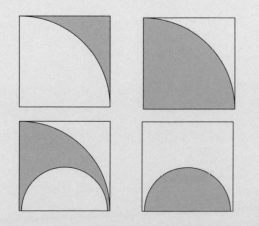

*Shapes from the Advanced Set*

## FABRIC REQUIREMENTS

$1^1/2$ yards focus fabric

### BACKGROUND FABRICS:

1 yard of a batik-type background fabric that will color-coordinate with your strata

1 yard watercolor-type background fabric

$1/8$ yard each of 3 additional background fabrics for the 3" blocks (optional) (pink, purple, and green were used in *Cycloid*)

$1/4$ yard of many fabrics for the strips (For *Cycloid* approximately 27 different fabrics were chosen.)

$1^1/2$ yards for the backing and sleeve

Batting: 38" square

## ASSEMBLY INSTRUCTIONS

**1.** Draft the Advanced Set of templates (see page 93) for the following block sizes: 3", 6", 9", 6" x 9", and 6" x 12" (see the templates on page 94 for the corner blocks).

**2.** Cut two $1^1/2$"-wide strips of all your fabrics. Arrange them from the lightest to the darkest on a design wall. Piece them into one large strata. Follow the sewing directions on page 24.

**3.** Mark the stripes created by the seams of the strata on your templates following the instructions on page 36.

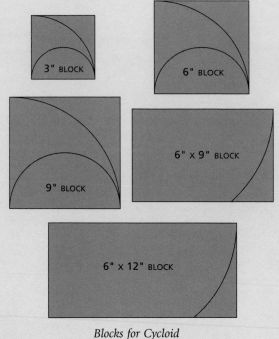

*Blocks for Cycloid*

Starting with the 3" blocks cut:

3" Quarter Circle: 26 of the focus fabric (Fussy cut these.)

3" L-Shapes: 29 from the 3 additional background fabrics

3" Wave: 3 from the focus fabric

3" Half Circle: 3 from the background fabrics

For the 6" blocks:

6" Quarter Circle: 6 total—2 from the focus fabric, 4 from strata

6" L-Shape: 8 from background fabrics

6" Wave: 2 total—1 from strata, 1 from focus fabric

6" Half Circle: 2 total—1 from strata, 1 from background fabrics

For the 9" blocks:

9" Quarter Circle: 3 from strata

9" L-Shape: 4 from background fabrics

9" Wave: 1 from strata

9" Half Circle: 1 from background fabrics

For the Connector blocks:

6" x 9" corner block: 1 from the batik-type background fabrics

6" x 12" corner block: 3 from the batik-type background fabrics

Small set-in curve: 4 from watercolor-type background fabrics

$3^1/2$" x $6^1/2$" stripped rectangles (cut from left-over strata): 8

$3^1/2$" square from batik-type background fabric: 1

**TIP**

In classes, students enjoyed more success with this quilt if they made their own choices for cutting the shapes. Cut all the shapes and arrange them on a design wall *before* you piece the blocks! This gives you a chance to audition all of the pieces of the quilt before piecing when there is still time to make color placement changes.

**4.** Refer to the quilt on page 82 to see where you may want to fussy cut the focus fabric.

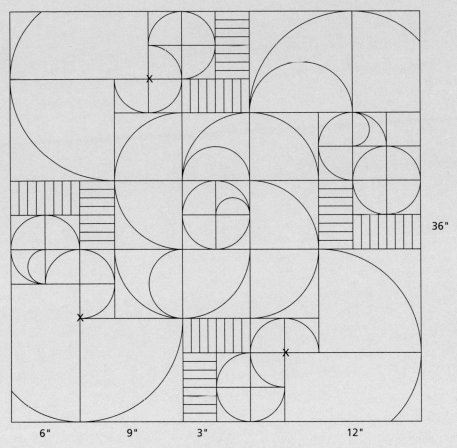

36"

6"    9"    3"    12"

*Quilt assembly diagram for* Cycloid

**5.** Now you can piece the different-sized blocks one at a time, always returning them to your design wall. This will make the piecing much easier later. You will have to piece some smaller sections to each other, so the piecing of this quilt top begins to make sense. Keep referring to your diagram.

- Piece the center—four 3" blocks.

- Make the center Nine-Patch by connecting the center blocks with the 6" blocks.

- Piece the 4 sections made up of the remaining 3" blocks and the connector blocks as shown in the diagram.

- Now connect the remaining 9" blocks and the 3 larger corner blocks. Notice that this last step is a little tricky because you will have to sew half seams in order to fit in the last pieces. These 3 spots are marked with an X in the assembly diagram.

Congratulations! The quilt top is together.

**6.** Layer the top, batting, and backing and baste the layers together.

**7.** Quilt as desired by hand or machine.

**8.** Bind with the focus fabric or any of the background fabrics.

**9.** Use any leftover strata to make a great label.

# RESOURCES

## Tools and Supplies

18" gridded Quilt and Sew Ruler (#96) by W.H. Collins Inc., Spartanburg, SC 29304 and See-Thru Drafting Ruler by The Quiltery *available through Prym-Dritz;* www.Dritz.com

Gridded template plastic by W.H. Collins (see above for address) or by EZ Quilting, Wrights, P.O. Box 398, West Warren, MA 01092-0398; 800-660-0415 or through www.threadart.com

Grifhold Yardstick Compass, Griffin Manufacturing Company, P.O. Box 308-C, Webster, NY 14580-0308; 716-265-1991

Sharpie Ultra Fine-Point Markers by Sanford Corporation, 2711 Washington Blvd., Bellwood, IL 60104; www.sanfordcorp.com

IRIS Swiss Super Fine Pins extra long $1^1/4$" by Gingham Square (item #NT438), available from www.quiltknit.com

Retayne by Pro Chem & Dye, P.O. Box 14, Somerset, MA 02726; 800-228-9393 or www.prochemical.com

Synthrapol (item #CHM1009) by Rupert, Gibbon & Spider, Inc., P.O. Box 425 Healdsburg, CA 95448-0425; 800-442-0455

Strips 'n Curves Cutting Basic Set templates (block size 9") by Quilt Escapes Inc., 4821 14th. Street SW, Loveland, CO 80537; 970-593-1265 or www.Quiltescapes.com

The Color Star (Color wheel) by Johannes Itten, Van Nostrand Reinhold, 115 Fifth Ave., New York, NY 10003; 800-926-2665 or http://catalog.wiley.com

The Designer I, Husqvarna Viking sewing machine; 800-358-0001 (for Canada call 800-461-5648) or www.husqvarnaviking.com

Quilt So Easy Discs (for ease in gripping and guiding the quilt while machine quilting) from Heavenly Notions, 4110 SE Hawthorne Blvd., Portland, OR 97214; 877-339-9339

For drafting the advanced set, Katie's Korners Radial Rule #118 by Katie Lane Quilts, PO Box 560408, Orlando, FL 32856-0408; (optional) Helpful in drafting curves in sizes $1^1/2$", 3", 4" and 6"; www.katielane.com

## Mail Order or Internet Sources

Hancock's of Paducah, 3841 Hinkleville Rd., Paducah, KY 42001; 800-845-8723 or www.Hancocks-Paducah.com (catalog available)

Keepsake Quilting, Rt. 25B, PO Box 1618, Centre Harbor, NH 03226; 800-865-9458 or www.keepsakequilting.com (catalog available)

Nancy's Notions, Box 683, Beaver Dam, WI 53916; 414-887-0690 (catalog available)

## Fabric

For fabrics online: www.eQuilter.com or call toll-free: 877-322-7423 (877-FABRIC-3)

Hand-painted fabrics by Fabrics-To-Dye-For, Two River Road, Pawcatuck, CT 06379; 888-322-1319 or www.FabricsToDyeFor.com

David Textiles, Inc., 5959 Telegraph Rd., City of Commerce, CA 90040; 323-728-3231

# BIBLIOGRAPHY

Anderson, Alex, *Rotary Cutting with Alex Anderson,* Lafayette, CA: C&T Publishing, 1999.

Gerritsen, Frans, *Evolution in Color,* West Chester, PA: Schiffer Publishing, Ltd., 1988.

Hassel, Kathleen A., *Super Quilter II* (Chapter 5, Understanding and Exploring Color), Lombard, IL: Wallace-Homestead Book Company, 1982.

Itten, Johannes, *The Elements of Color,* New York: Van Nostrand Reinhold, 1970.

McKelvey, Susan, *A Quilter's Guide to Creative Ideas for Color and Fabric,* New York: Rodale Press, 1998.

Penders, Mary Coyne, *Color & Cloth,* San Francisco, CA: The Quilt Digest Press, 1995.

Perry, Gai, *Color from the Heart,* Lafayette, CA: C&T Publishing, 1999.

Salemme, Lucia A., *Color Exercises for the Painter,* New York: Watson-Guptill, 1975.

Westray, Kathleen, *A Color Sampler,* New York: Ticknor & Fields, 1993.

Wolfrom, Joen, *Color Play: Easy Steps to Imaginative Color in Quilts,* Lafayette, CA: C&T Publishing, 2000.

Wolfrom, Joen, *The Magical Effects of Color* (my personal favorite) Lafayette, CA: C&T Publishing, 1992.

For free color lessons on the Internet log on to: http://www.quiltwoman.com/workshop.html

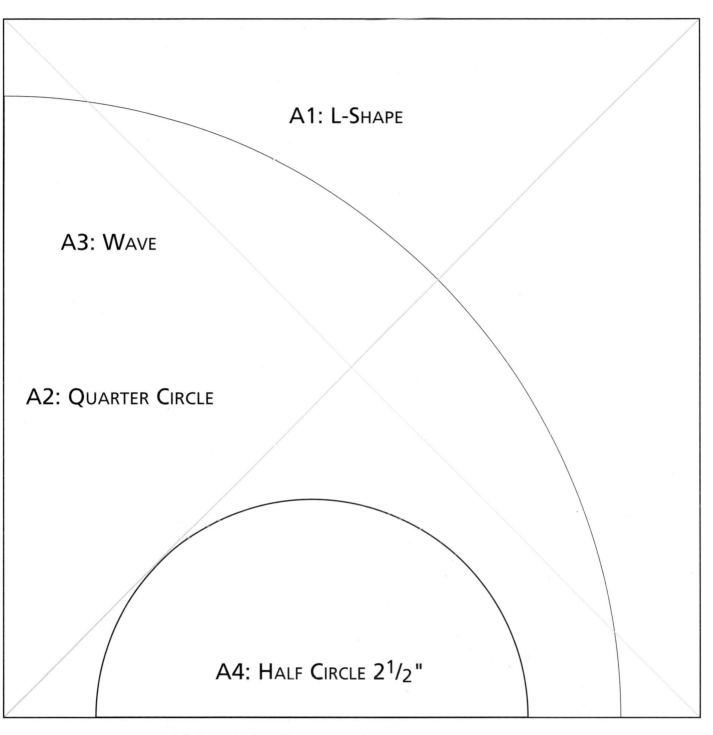

A1: L-Shape

A3: Wave

A2: Quarter Circle

A4: Half Circle 2$^1$/$_2$"

8" Basic Set Template Pattern (Enlarge 110%)

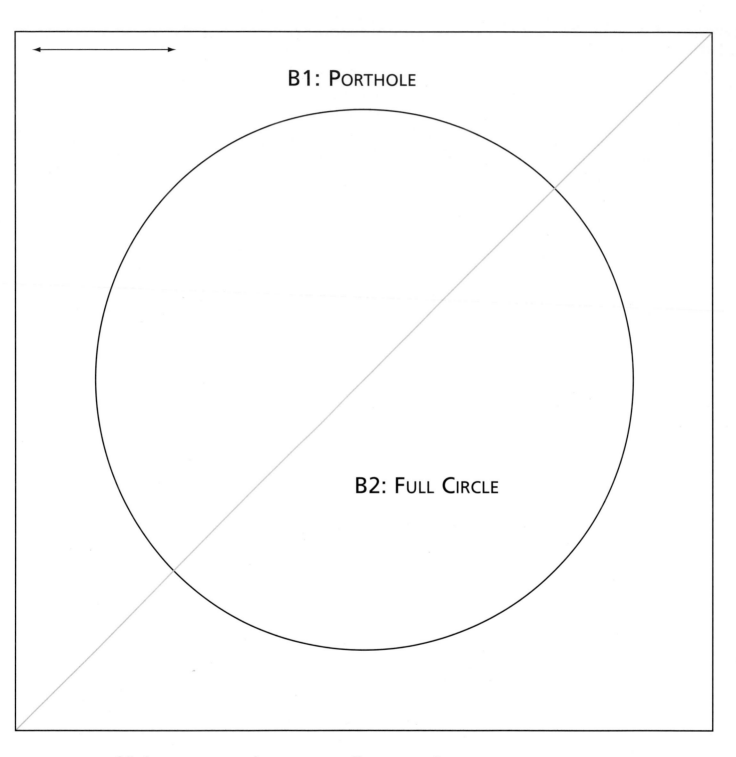

**B1: PORTHOLE**

**B2: FULL CIRCLE**

## 8" SQUARE AND PORTHOLE TEMPLATE PATTERNS (Enlarge 110%)

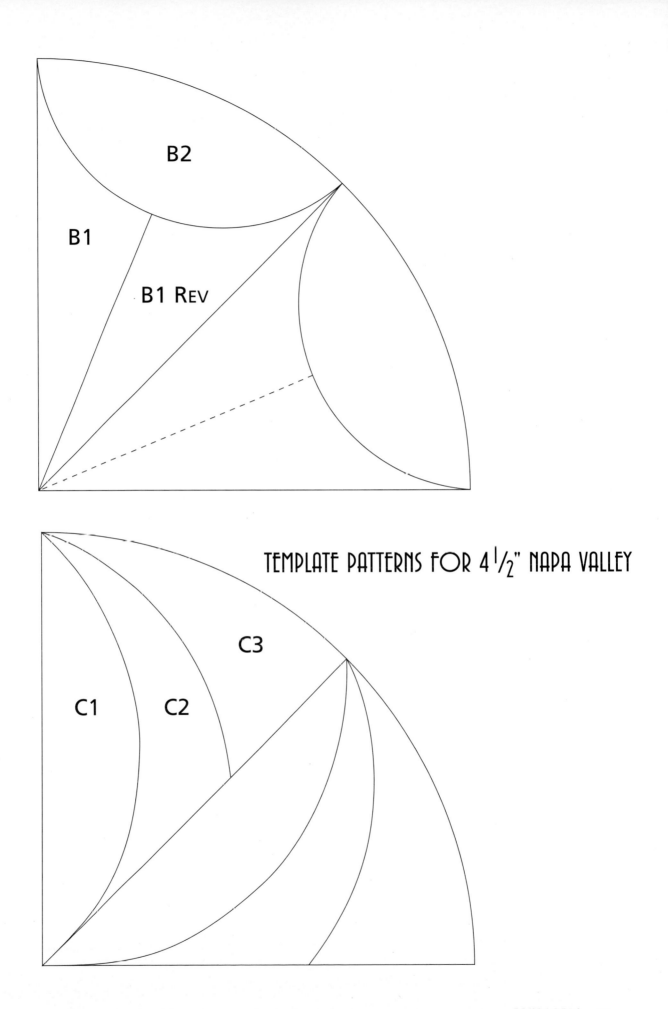

B2

B1

B1 Rᴇᴠ

TEMPLATE PATTERNS FOR 4 ¹/₂" NAPA VALLEY

C3

C1

C2

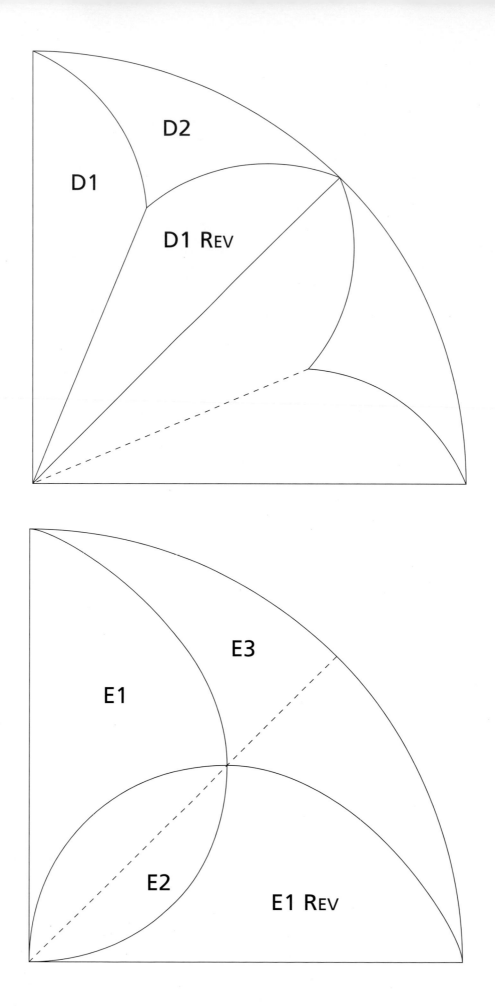

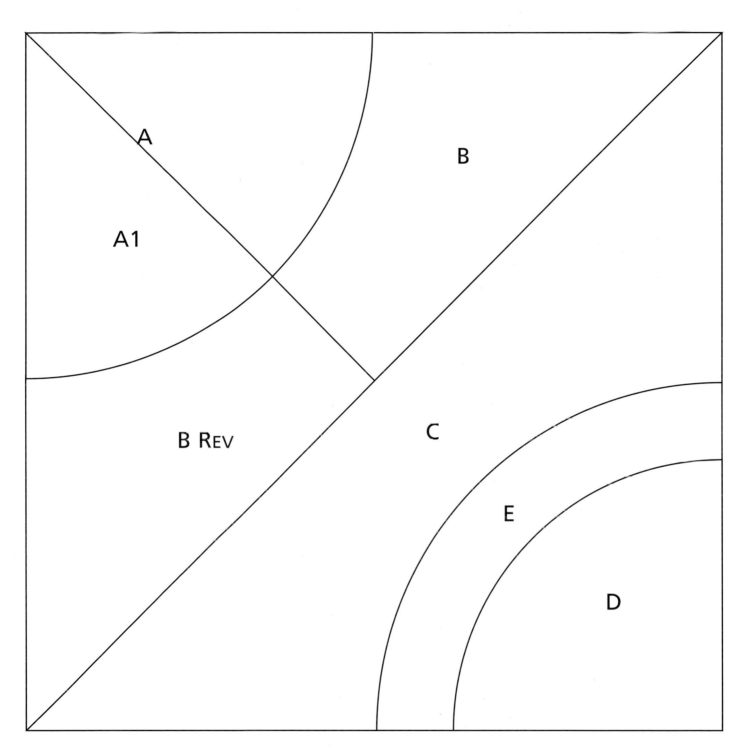

**8" Negative/Positive Templates** (Enlarge 110%)

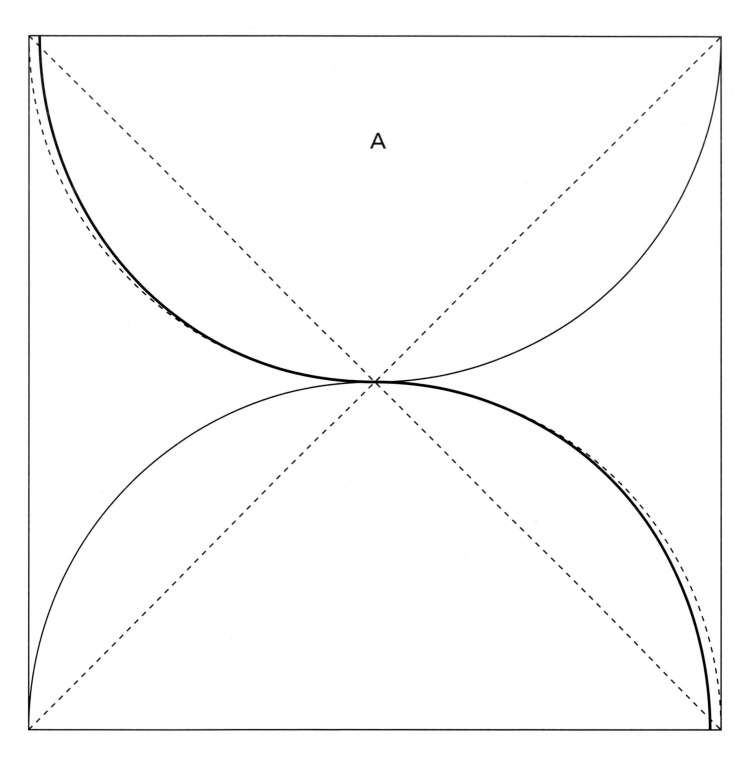

A

8" Flowing Ribbons Template (Enlarge 110%)

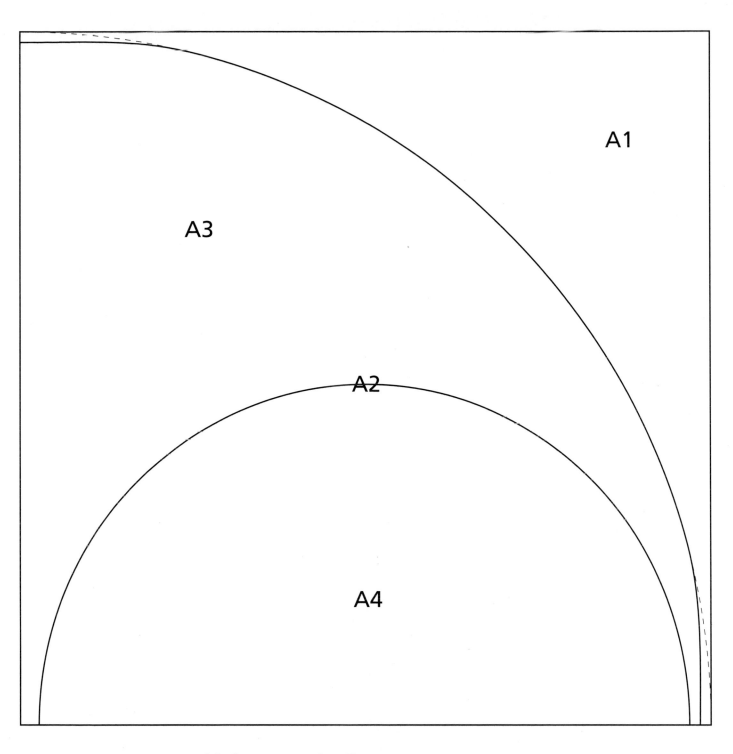

**8" Advanced Set Templates** (Enlarge 110%)

# Template Patterns for *Cycloid* Corner Blocks

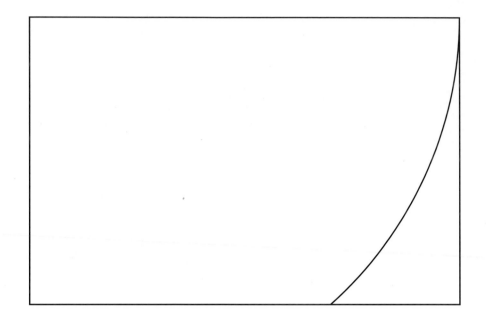

**6" x 9" Template** (Enlarge 200%)

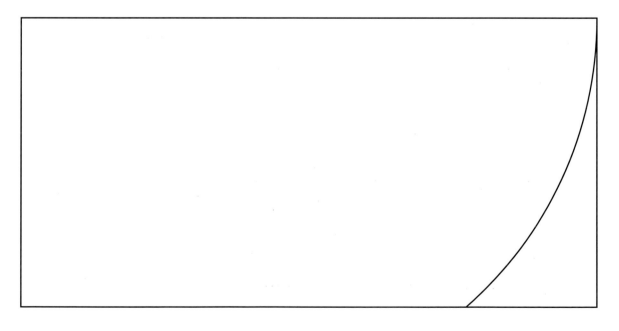

**6" x 12" Template** (Enlarge 200%)

## ABOUT THE AUTHOR

Born in Indonesia, where the fabulous batiks of the region kindled a life-long love of fabric, Louisa Smith was educated in the Netherlands. There, her years of appreciation for the needle arts began. Upon moving to the United States in 1960, she was immediately drawn to quilting and quickly became an accomplished devotee. Her love of antique quilts led her to one- and two-patch designs. These traditional shapes are her inspiration for new and unique designs. Working with fabric, color, and design is what Louisa enjoys most.

Louisa lives with her husband and mother in Loveland, Colorado.

If you are interested in Louisa's workshops and lectures you can write to her at:

4821 14th Street SW, Loveland, CO 80537
or visit her website www.Quiltescapes.com

## INDEX

### Subject Index

Background fabrics, 16, 17-18
Borders, 55
Circles:
   appliquéing, 44, 50-51, 53
   designing with, 42, 45
   Interlocking Circles, 70-73
Color wheel, 12, 13
Complementary colors, 14
Drafting the templates, see Templates
Embellishing, 54-55
Fabric, 10
Fat quarters, 16
Focal point, 44
Focus fabric, 15
Marking, 36, 48
Miniature Strips 'n Curves, 25, 65-66
Mismatched strips, 49
Mock-ups, fabric, 20
Monochromatic color scheme, 13
Piecing tips, 48-49
Pinning, 48
Polychromatic color scheme, 14
Pressing, 25, 49, 54
Prewashing, 10, 21
Quilting, 58-59
Quilt top, assembling, 54
Scale of prints, 17
Seam allowance, 24
Sewing tips for strata, 24
Strata, 10, 21-25
Strips, cutting, 21
Tools/supplies, 10-11
Transition fabrics, 16
Value, 16, 40

### Templates:

Advanced Set, 32, 34, 39
Basic Set II, 30-31
Basic Set, 26-29, 87, 88
Beg and Borrow, 60-62
Cutting apart, 37
Cutting shapes with, 37
Flowing Ribbons, 67-69, 92
Marking, 36
Mini, 65-66
Napa Valley 4$^1/_2$", 89
Negative/Positive, 64-65, 91
Patterns, 87-94

### Quilt Index

*Arco Iris* (Amy Robertson), 62
*Aurora* (Louisa Smith), 66
*Bermuda High* (Virginia Pollenz), 9
*Blossom* (Janet Duncan Dignan), 44
*Chop Sticks* (Louisa Smith), 70
*Citrus Flavor* (Louisa Smith), 74
*Colorado Sunset* (Louisa Smith), 78, 79
*Color Infusion* (Louisa Smith), 55
*Colours of St. Lucia* (Dennie A. Sullivan), 54
*Connections: a.k.a. I Can't Believe It Lies Flat* (Kimberly White), 19
*Connections* (Louisa Smith), 31
*Cycloid* (Louisa Smith), 82
*Cycloid II* (Louisa Smith), 6, 46
*Donna's Blue Galaxy* (Mary L. Penton), 61
*Dreamscape* (Amy Robertson), 27
*Drifting Apart* (Michele Koppelman), 73
*Dr. Watson's Cosmos* (Marilyn Eimon), 12, 52
*Fifth Rock from the Sun* (Frances Andersen Rosenfeld), 29

*Flutterby* (Linda Coughlin), 15
*Garam Masala* (Amy Robertson), 35
*Grace* (Marion Connors), 34
*Hawaiian Holiday* (Louisa Smith), 67
*Hawaiian Holiday II* (Louisa Smith), 67
*Key Lime Pie* (Carol Wight Jones), 65
*Looking Thru the Stratasphere* (Gwyned Trefethen), 71
*Mango Sunset* (Carol E. Dexter), 45
*Moon Dance* (Carol Wight Jones), 33
*Moongazing* (Cathy Clay), 58
*Napa Valley* (Louisa Smith), 63
*Nature's Splendor* (Paula DiMattei), 41
*Night Lights* (Jo McCoy), 57
*Norwegian Sunset* (Michele Koppelman), 38
*Purple Haze* (Vicki Carlson), 68
*Reflections of Provence* (Louisa Smith), 45
*Rhythm of the Islands* (Louisa Smith), 14
*Ripples* (Cathy Granese), 13
*Round About* (Louisa Smith), 30
*Serenity* (Louisa Smith), 46
*Stratasphere* (Carol Wight Jones), 56
*Summer Rain* (Marion Connors), 62
*Sun Kissed* (Louisa Smith), 43
*Sunset in the Japanese Garden* (Louisa Smith), 22
*Sunset at Serengeti* (Jodi Davila), 29
*Tropicana* (Louisa Smith), 8
*Un Dia de Guanacaste* (Amy Robertson), 47
*Winner's Circle* (Louisa Smith), 72

## Other Fine Books From C&T Publishing:

*250 Continuous-Line Quilting Designs for Hand, Machine & Long-Arm Quilters*, Laura Lee Fritz

*Along the Garden Path: More Quilters and Their Gardens*, Jean and Valori Wells

*The Art of Machine Piecing: Quality Workmanship Through a Colorful Journey*, Sally Collins

*The Art of Classic Quiltmaking*, Harriet Hargrave and Sharyn Craig

*The Best of Baltimore Beauties*, Elly Sienkiewicz

*Block Magic: Over 50 Fun & Easy Blocks made from Squares and Rectangles*, Nancy Johnson-Srebro

*Color From the Heart: Seven Great Ways to Make Quilts with Colors You Love*, Gai Perry

*Color Play: Easy Steps to Imaginative Color in Quilts*, Joen Wolfrom

*Cotton Candy Quilts: Using Feedsacks, Vintage and Reproduction Fabrics*, Mary Mashuta

*Curves in Motion: Quilt Designs & Techniques*, Judy B. Dales

*Cut-Loose Quilts: Stack, Slice, Switch & Sew*, Jan Mullen

*Diane Phalen Quilts: 10 Projects to Celebrate the Seasons*, Diane Phalen

*Do-It-Yourself Framed Quilts: Fast, Fun & Easy Projects*, Gai Perry

*Exploring Machine Trapunto: New Dimensions*, Hari Walner

*Fabric Shopping with Alex Anderson, Seven Projects to Help You: Make Successful Choices, Build Your Confidence, Add to Your Fabric Stash*, Alex Anderson

*Fantastic Fabric Folding: Innovative Quilting Projects*, Rebecca Wat

*Flower Pounding: Quilt Projects for All Ages*, Amy Sandrin & Ann Frischkorn

*Free Stuff for Quilters on the Internet, 3rd Ed.*, Judy Heim and Gloria Hansen

*Free Stuff for Sewing Fanatics on the Internet*, Judy Heim and Gloria Hansen

*Free Stuff for Stitchers on the Internet*, Judy Heim and Gloria Hansen

*Free Stuff for Traveling Quilters on the Internet*, Gloria Hansen

*Free-Style Quilts: A "No Rules" Approach*, Susan Carlson

*Ghost Layers & Color Washes: Three Steps to Spectacular Quilts*, Katie Pasquini Masopust

*Great Lakes, Great Quilts: 12 Projects Celebrating Quilting Traditions*, Marsha MacDowell

*Hand Appliqué with Alex Anderson: Seven Projects for Hand Appliqué*, Alex Anderson

*Hand Quilting with Alex Anderson: Six Projects for Hand Quilters*, Alex Anderson

*Heirloom Machine Quilting, Third Edition*, Harriet Hargrave

*In the Nursery: Creative Quilts and Designer Touches*, Jennifer Sampou & Carolyn Schmitz

*Laurel Burch Quilts: Kindred Creatures*, Laurel Burch

*Lone Star Quilts and Beyond: Projects and Inspiration*, Jan Krentz

*Machine Embroidery and More: Ten Step-by-Step Projects Using Border Fabrics & Beads*, Kristen Dibbs

*Magical Four-Patch and Nine-Patch Quilts*, Yvonne Porcella

*Make Any Block Any Size*, Joen Wolfrom

*On the Surface: Thread Embellishment & Fabric Manipulation*, Wendy Hill

*The Photo Transfer Handbook: Snap It, Print It, Stitch It!*, Jean Ray Laury

*Pieced Flowers*, Ruth B. McDowell

*Piecing: Expanding the Basics*, Ruth B. McDowell

*Quilted Memories: Celebrations of Life*, Mary Lou Weidman

*The Quilted Garden: Design & Make Nature-Inspired Quilts*, Jane A. Sassaman

*Quilting Back to Front: Fun & Easy No-Mark Techniques*, Larraine Scouler

*Quilting with Carol Armstrong: 30 Quilting Patterns, Appliqué Designs, 16 Projects*, Carol Armstrong

*Quilts for Guys: 15 Fun Projects For Your Favorite Fella*

*Rotary Cutting with Alex Anderson: Tips, Techniques, and Projects*, Alex Anderson

*Shadow Redwork™ with Alex Anderson: 24 Designs to Mix and Match*, Alex Anderson

*Smashing Sets: Exciting Ways to Arrange Quilt Blocks*, Margaret J. Miller

*Snowflakes & Quilts*, Paula Nadelstern

*Start Quilting with Alex Anderson, 2nd Edition: Six Projects for First-Time Quilters*, Alex Anderson

*Stitch 'n Flip Quilts: 14 Fantastic Projects*, Valori Wells

*A Thimbleberries Housewarming: 22 Projects for Quilters.* Lynette Jensen

*Through the Garden Gate: Quilters and Their Gardens*, Jean and Valori Wells

*Two-for-One Foundation Piecing: Reversible Quilts and More*, Wendy Hill

*For more information write for a free catalog:*
C&T Publishing, Inc.
P.O. Box 1456
Lafayette, CA 94549
(800) 284-1114
e-mail: ctinfo@ctpub.com
website: www.ctpub.com

*For quilting supplies:*
Cotton Patch Mail Order
3405 Hall Lane, Dept. CTB
Lafayette, CA 94549
(800) 835-4418
(925) 283-7883
e-mail: quiltusa@yahoo.com
website: www.quiltusa.com